APPLIQUÉ
MASTERPIECE

LITTLE
BROWN BIRD

Patterns

Margaret Docherty

American Quilter's Society

P. O. Box 3290 • Paducah, KY 42002-3290

Located in Paducah, Kentucky, the American Quilter's Society (AQS) is dedicated to promoting the accomplishments of today's quilters. Through its publications and events, AQS strives to honor today's quiltmakers and their work and to inspire future creativity and innovation in quiltmaking.

EDITOR: BARBARA SMITH
BOOK DESIGN/ILLUSTRATIONS: ELAINE WILSON
COVER DESIGN: MICHAEL BUCKINGHAM
PHOTOGRAPHY: CHARLES R. LYNCH

Library of Congress Cataloging-in-Publication Data
Docherty, Margaret.
        Appliqué masterpiece : little brown bird patterns / Margaret Docherty.
        p. cm.
        Includes bibliographical references and index.
        ISBN 1-57432-734-8
        1. Appliqué--Patterns. 2. Quilting--Patterns. 3. Quilts I. Title: Little brown bird
        patterns. II. Title.

        TT779.C63 1999
        746.46'041--dc21   99-056546

Additional copies of this book may be ordered from the American Quilter's Society, PO Box 3290, Paducah, KY 42002-3290 @ $21.95. Add $2.00 for postage and handling.

Copyright © 2000, Margaret Docherty

Dedication

To TBD with love from MEG

Acknowledgments

To Creana Roberts for taking hundreds of pages of rough manuscript and turning them into the basis of a book.

To Brian for his typing, his photography, and his cooking.

Contents

Preface

As with many quilters, it was the fabrics that first got me hooked. The colors, the designs, the textures held enough appeal in their own right, but the justification for buying and possessing them came from putting them to use by turning them into quilts. That was back in the late '80s, and now, not a day goes by without my doing some quilting.

I work as a pediatrician, and each night after dinner, I do a crossword puzzle and sew for about six hours. Perhaps my liking for puzzles explains my love of quilting, but possibly it's just that you can get an awful lot of fabrics into one quilt!

I did puzzle out most of the techniques for myself, and a few lessons would have made the learning curve less steep. So I have written this book for a number of reasons. First of all, my quilt Little Brown Bird was kindly received both in the United Kingdom and the United States, and I have had many inquiries about the methods I have used. Second, I felt that because I was self-taught, I might be able to help some of you avoid the pot-holes I have fallen into from time to time. Third, I enjoyed the writing of it, and finally, if I sell enough copies, I can cut back on the day job, do more crossword puzzles, and make more quilts.

I hope the instructions are helpful. They are not meant to be "gospel" but are intended as a guide for both beginners and experimenters. Whatever your level of skill or interest, I hope you get as much pleasure from re-creating the blocks from Brown Bird and designing your own versions as I did.

Margaret Docherty

LITTLE BROWN BIRD

Margaret Docherty

Introduction

LITTLE BROWN BIRD measures 84" wide by 84½" long. It was started Easter 1994 and completed in the early summer of 1997. Between August 1995 and February 1996, the quilt was put aside. The total time spent working on it was two and a half years.

An inscription is inked on the back:

Little Brown Bird so lonely,
All your playmates have flown,
Tell me why are you flying
Round the hedge all alone?

Dear Rosebush I'm hungry,
My dinner I seek
Won't you spare me a hip
With a bright scarlet cheek?

This is a favorite song from nursery years, but in this quilt, my Brown Bird is neither lonely nor hungry. A small appliqué of a wren on a branch of rose hips accompanies the inscription. Wrens appear in the quilt in Block 17 and in the center of each border.

Margaret Docherty

CHAPTER 1

Fabric Selection

Margaret Docherty

All the fabric used for Little Brown Bird, including the batting, is 100% cotton. I purchased yardage specifically for the background, borders, and sashings, and all the rest came from my store of fabrics. The greatest pleasure in making this quilt was the discovery that I had on hand many of the fabrics I needed to give me just the effect I was looking for. I don't believe that many quilters past the novice stage will need to purchase all the fabric necessary for this quilt. Most of us have cupboards full of the stuff! Just in case someone hasn't, I will make some suggestions for fabric selection. For necessary yardage, see Chapter 5.

For the background, I used a fabric called "Tan Teapot Print." It has brownish splotches on a dark cream background, so it resembles a poor attempt at tea dyeing. It has that look of age about it that inspires immediate affection. In fact, Juliet Webster, of the Patchwork Association in England, saw work in progress on this quilt and kept asking me, "How are you getting on with that old thing you found in the attic?"

There are many such fabrics on the market, or you may prefer a clean, fresh background, a white on white, or white on cream calico, for example. Another choice would be a chintzy look. A pastel small print calico would be ideal. It would be interesting to see the quilt made up with a more modern setting of bright colors on a solid black or navy background.

There are no home made tie-dyed fabrics in the quilt, but I have used scraps of those I've purchased from professional hand dyers. All of the roses and some of the leaves were cut from one piece of a perfectly hideous tie-dye purchased at a well-known English department store. It is shown in Fabric 11 and can be seen in the roses in Block 6, Rose Basket. Once I realized how useful it was going to be, I tried to buy some more, but alas, they were sold out. I hate to think for what other purpose this fabric has been used.

Little Brown Bird quilt

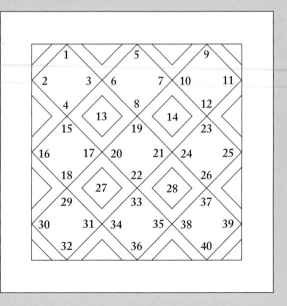

Block numbers and placement

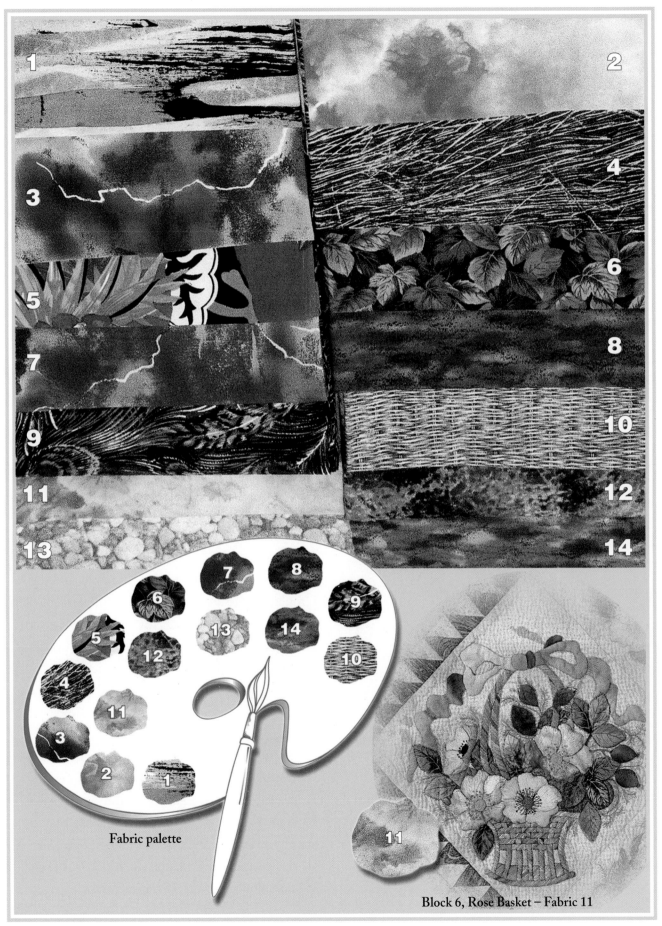

Fabric palette

Block 6, Rose Basket – Fabric 11

Margaret Docherty

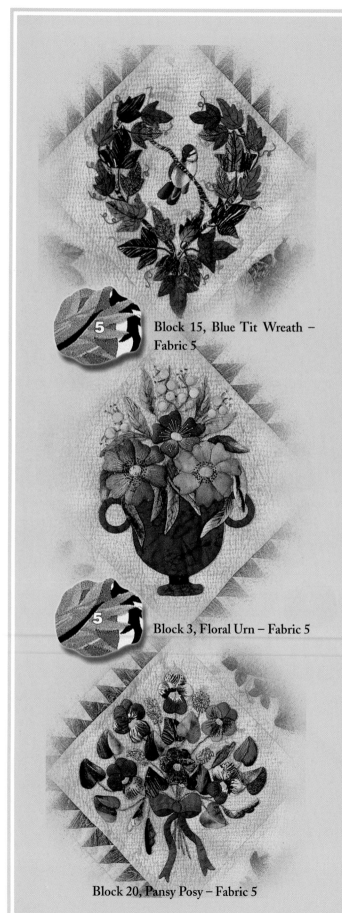

Block 15, Blue Tit Wreath – Fabric 5

Block 3, Floral Urn – Fabric 5

Block 20, Pansy Posy – Fabric 5

Most of the appliqué fabric was commercially produced prints to give texture and value. I purposely search for fabrics that have no definite pattern but have a good variety of values of one hue or multiple colors. With a good selection of fabrics and a plastic template, I can "paint" in a way I certainly couldn't manage with a paint box and brushes.

The birds in this quilt are a good example of improvisation. The blue tit in Block 15, Blue Tit Wreath, was cut from a French cotton, Fabric 5, with a large-scale pattern, which also served as leaves in Block 3, Floral Urn, and for some of the violas in Block 20, Pansy Posy. I named the quilt for the wren that appears in Block 17, Little Brown Bird, and in the center of each border. His breast is not carefully painted. It was cut from a fabric depicting stones, Fabric 13.

The bullfinch in Block 18, Bullfinch Ring, was cut from a modern Bali-type material, Fabric 1. The black head and mottled back were cut as one piece, with another area of the fabric providing the tail and underbody.

The love birds in Block 35, Victorian Love Birds, were cut from one piece of fabric, and the templates were arranged to give a different color for the head and breast. Any resemblance to a pair of male chaffinches (European finches) is purely coincidental. A fabric depicting large feathers was widely used, at different angles, for tails, backs, and wings, Fabric 9.

I used an identical fabric in two colorways – dark red and yellow for berries, and green and yellow for the main fabric for the leaves, Fabrics 8 and 14, Block 17. Fabrics 3 and 7, also two separate colorways, were used for some of the anemones in Block 22, Bowl of Anemones, and all the cosmos-type flowers in Block 9, Heart Wreath, and Block 12, Cosmos Swirl.

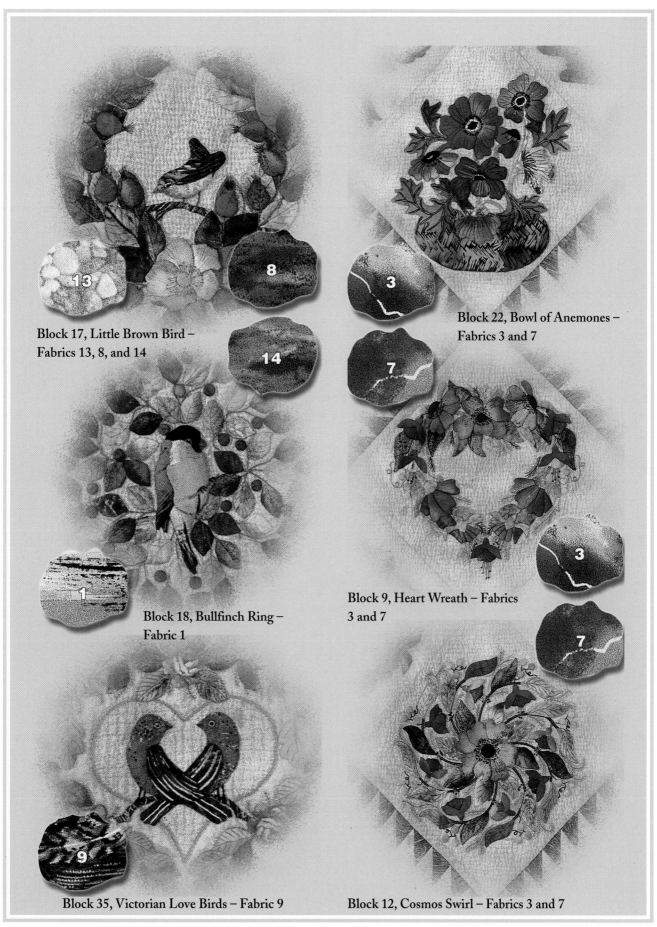

Block 17, Little Brown Bird –
Fabrics 13, 8, and 14

Block 18, Bullfinch Ring –
Fabric 1

Block 22, Bowl of Anemones –
Fabrics 3 and 7

Block 9, Heart Wreath – Fabrics
3 and 7

Block 35, Victorian Love Birds – Fabric 9

Block 12, Cosmos Swirl – Fabrics 3 and 7

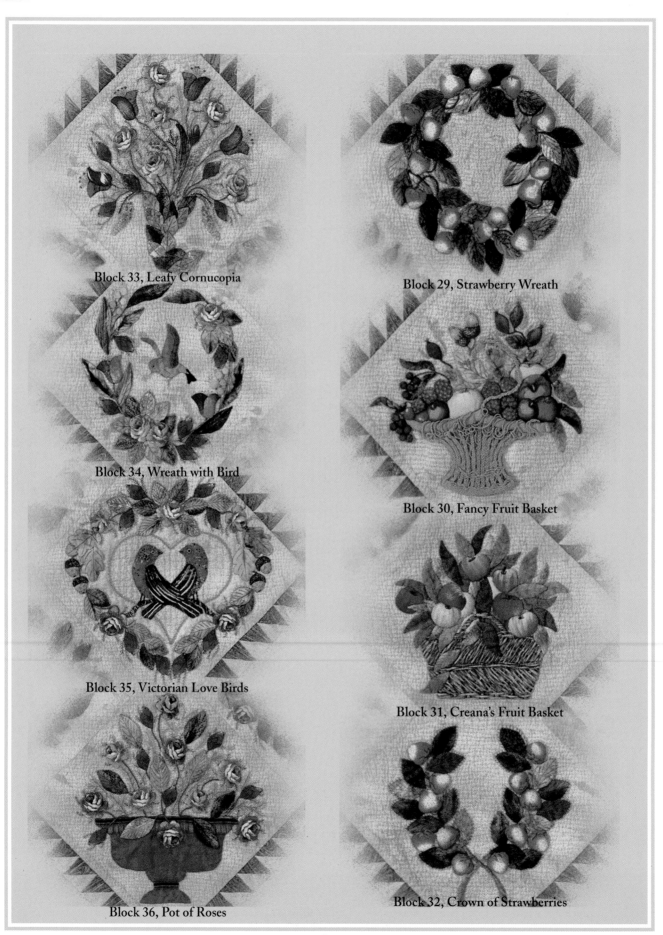

Block 33, Leafy Cornucopia

Block 29, Strawberry Wreath

Block 34, Wreath with Bird

Block 30, Fancy Fruit Basket

Block 35, Victorian Love Birds

Block 31, Creana's Fruit Basket

Block 36, Pot of Roses

Block 32, Crown of Strawberries

In some areas, I have used broderie perse, for example, the small roses in Blocks 33–36 and the fruit in Blocks 29–32. The most useful find in my cupboard was a three-yard remnant of a bargain misprint fabric, from which I cut all the rosebuds.

The leaves for the border were another source of great enjoyment. I used about 50 different fabrics and attempted to manipulate more than one hue or value into each separate appliqué leaf.

There is a wide variety of fabrics currently available resembling twigs, bark, grasses, baskets, etc. I utilized a selection of these for stems and baskets (see Fabrics 4 and 10 in Block 2). The brown fabric of the narrow borders, sashings, and sawtooth borders resembles tree bark, and it enhanced the rustic look I wanted.

The second narrow border is a Bali-type intense blue, which was chosen as an accent. Blue is the least used color in the quilt blocks.

The scherenschnitte, Blocks 13, 14, 27, and 28, stand alone rather than in groups of four and need a strong dark color. I used my berry fabric, Fabric 8, for two of them, and the other two were worked in a wonderful autumnal brown and yellow fabric designed by Nancy Crow, Fabric 12, page 16.

Tie-dyed fabrics were used for the cyclamen and some ribbons, Fabric 2. Tie-dyes, along with commercial marble-look fabrics, are good for pots and vases.

Because no two blocks in this quilt are alike, small scraps of many fabrics will suffice. I used a degree of continuity for the border in that all the flowers are roses, but you may decide to vary the flowers or even use broderie perse.

Corner of border with sample of leaves

Block 2, Basket of Poppies – Fabrics 4, 10, and 2

Block 13, Appliqué Feather – Fabric 8

Block 14, Imitation Scherenschnitte – Fabric 12

Block 27, Scherenschnitte 1 – Fabric 12

Block 28, Scherenschnitte 2 – Fabric 8

CHAPTER 2

Neat & Tidy Hand Appliqué

This chapter covers finger-pressing and needle-turn appliqué. Good hand appliqué has smooth curves, sharp points, and almost invisible stitching.

Mark Background Fabric

A light box is helpful for transferring your designs to the background fabric. Test your marker on a scrap of background fabric to make sure it can be seen and easily removed. A water-soluble pen can be used for light fabrics and a white or silver quilter's pencil for dark fabrics.

Make Templates

See-through plastic has many benefits. It is easy to transfer markings from the original paper design to the plastic. Just position the plastic on top of the paper pattern and draw. Use a fine-point, permanent marker.

Plastic templates are durable and can be used over and over again. Because you can see through them, you can choose portions of a fabric that will enhance your appliqué, creating such effects as the markings on a leaf or the shadings of a petal.

When marking your plastic, attach it to your paper pattern with masking tape so that it does not slip. Because a plastic template can easily be mislaid, make a duplicate template or keep a container for templates close at hand whenever you are using one.

Fine embroidery scissors are good for cutting out templates. Remember to cut nice smooth edges and check the shape. Your finished appliqué will reflect the quality of the template. Try drawing around a new template on a piece of paper to check the shape and evenness before using it on fabric. Don't compromise. If it is not good enough, make another.

Prepare Fabric

Prewash your fabrics and check for colorfastness. Then starch your chosen fabric with spray starch. This is a very important step. There are three advantages to starched versus unstarched fabric. The extra stiffness of starched fabric makes it easier to finger press your appliqué pieces, giving them crisper edges and making them less likely to stretch. Starched fabric is less likely to fray. With a small piece of appliqué, you get a second chance if your first attempt at finger pressing is not accurate or if you need to manipulate your points. Marking the fabric for appliqué shapes is easier, too. The starch holds the piece steady, and a lead pencil gives a cleaner mark on starched fabric.

Mark Fabric

Rest your fabric on a sheet of fine sandpaper, either on an old table or on top of a cutting mat if you are working on a surface you care about. Smooth the fabric out, right side up, and try your template on several areas of the fabric to decide which has the most pleasing effect. Mark carefully around the template. A fine mechanical lead pencil is ideal, whenever it's possible to use one. If a fabric is resistant to being marked, you may need to use a heavier pencil, such as one with a 2B lead.

If you are marking several patches on one piece of fabric, be sure to leave plenty of space between them. Remember appliqué templates *do not include turn-under allowances*. If in doubt, draw a faint pencil line, free-hand, about ¼" all around the marked appliqué piece and reposition your template another ¼" away from that line before marking your next shape (Fig. 2–1).

Cut Fabric

Rough-cut fabric shapes with scissors, leaving a generous turn-under allowance, which can be trimmed later.

Trim, Clip, Press

Having rough-cut all the appliqué pieces for one block, you need to give them a little more attention before they can be stitched in place on the background fabric. Trim turn-under allowances neatly. A ¼" allowance is fine for large pieces, but small shapes will need only ⅛" to ³⁄₁₆". A generous use of spray starch will give you more confidence here. Don't trim the allowance too closely at the points, and don't cut it off completely.

A gentle curve, such as the A curve in Fig. 2–2, will need less drastic clipping than an acute curve like B. Uniformly spaced clips, spaced close together, will give a smoother fold line than notches will (Fig. 2–3).

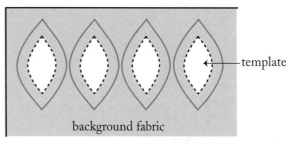

background fabric

allow generous seam allowance

Fig. 2–1.

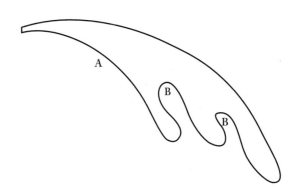

Fig. 2–2.

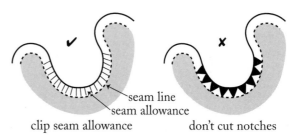

clip seam allowance   don't cut notches

Fig. 2–3.

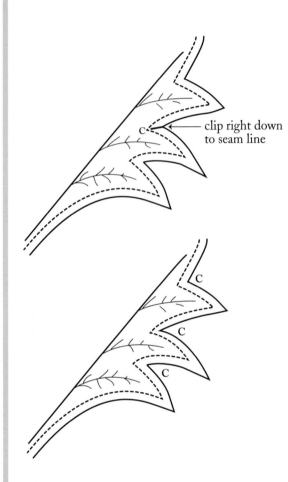

clip right down
to seam line

FIG. 2–4.

FIG. 2–5.

A very tight angle, such as the C's in Fig. 2–4, will need to be clipped right down to the line, and the amount of allowance should fade away to nothing. To prevent fraying, a small drop of a fray inhibitor can be applied in the area. The finest paint brush you can find is ideal for this purpose.

Using your finger and thumb, press the turn-under allowance to the wrong side. Aim to have your pressed line just inside the marked line so that all pencil marks will be hidden in the allowance.

A gentle concave curve, well-starched and clipped, will finger press beautifully into place and cause no problems during stitching. Take care when pressing convex curves, such as the D's in Fig. 2–5.

Press one small area at a time, never allowing the fullness in the allowance to fall into creases, which will show up as little points on the finished stitched appliqué. Also, be careful not to stretch the allowances.

Stitch

Baste the appliqué pieces one at a time, using the basting method of your choice; for example, you could use fabric glue. You could thread baste through the center of a piece, leaving the edges free, or you could use pins (inserted from the wrong side of the background fabric to avoid catching your thread).

Try to match the position of your piece as accurately as possible to its corresponding placement markings on the background fabric. Don't worry if your pressed allowances spring out. The starch has given you a good fold line that can easily be turned under again as you sew.

Needles and Thread

Quilting "betweens," needle size 10 or 12, are recommended, but the choice is a personal one. Appliqué needles, called "sharps," are slightly longer than betweens, and they are readily available at quilting-supply shops.

Select a sewing thread that matches the color of the appliqué piece. To see if the thread matches your fabric, hold a length of thread over the fabric and stand back a couple of feet. The thread should blend into the background and be barely visible. If possible, try several threads before deciding. You really will make life difficult for yourself if your thread is several shades lighter than your fabric.

I remember my grandmother advising me to select a thread a shade darker than the fabric because "threads always work in lighter." I've found this to be true. This may sound like a trivial piece of advice, but it is a most important part of stitching.

Starting Knot

Many people are taught to start appliquéing by bringing a knotted thread from the wrong side of the appliqué piece through to the right side in the edge of the fold (Fig. 2–6). This method has two drawbacks. The knots may not hold, and they can stand out as a bump in an otherwise smooth appliqué.

Instead, try taking three or four tiny stitches in the right side of the background fabric in an area that will be hidden under the appliqué (Fig. 2–7). Then push your needle through to the wrong side of the background fabric and bring it up through to the right side and on into the folded edge of the appliqué piece (Fig. 2–8).

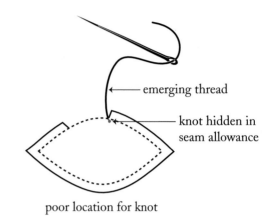

emerging thread

knot hidden in seam allowance

poor location for knot

FIG. 2–6.

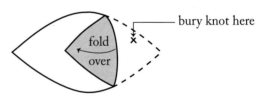

bury knot here

fold over

better location for knot

FIG. 2–7.

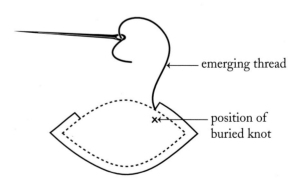

emerging thread

position of buried knot

FIG. 2–8.

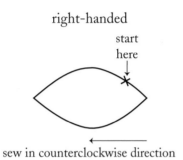

right-handed

start here

sew in counterclockwise direction

left-handed

start here

sew in clockwise direction

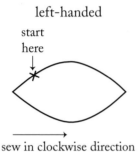

FIG. 2–9.

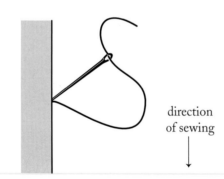

direction of sewing

FIG. 2–10.

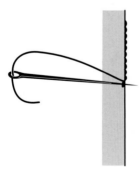

FIG. 2–11.

THE APPLIQUÉ STITCH

Note: The position for knotting and the direction of sewing depend on whether you are right- or left-handed (Fig. 2–9).

The closer together your stitches are, the better the final result will be. This is particularly true for areas where there is fullness to be eased, as for convex curves. Insert the needle into the background just underneath the appliqué to produce stitches that are nicely buried (Fig. 2–10).

The thread should be pulled firmly enough to bury the stitch but not so tightly that it causes an obvious indentation in the fabric. When you press the finished piece, because the stitches have been inserted underneath, the piece will press very flat, nearly hiding the stitches.

ENDING KNOT

To avoid lumpy ending knots, overlap your beginning stitch by one or two stitches. Take your needle down through the appliqué, as close as possible to the emerging thread (Fig. 2–11). Make three or four small stitches in the background fabric to finish (Fig. 2–12).

Needle-Turning

This term is used to describe using your sewing needle to turn under the allowance ahead of your needle as you stitch. With nicely starched and finger-pressed folds, this is easy to do along shallow curves and straight lines. But what about curves where the fullness in the allowance has to be neatly hidden without causing bumps and creases on the right side? What about all the excess fabric protruding around sharp points? Here, "needle turning" is rather a misnomer. Unless you are stitching with something resembling a poker, your needle is not strong enough to do the job required of it. To turn your fabric under, try a large, stout needle with a sharp point, or a short, stout pin. They are natural choices for fine appliqué work involving small complex shapes. These special turning needles can be kept close at hand by inserting them into your background fabric.

Full (Convex) Curves

To avoid bumps and creases on the finished fold line, keep your stitches very close together and constantly re-align the fold so you can sweep any fullness into the area already stitched. On a very full curve, re-align the fold every one or two stitches. Smooth curves come with practice, patience, and good preparation.

For the following method for handling convex curves, you will need at least a ³⁄₁₆" turn-under allowance. For the example in Fig. 2–13, stitch until you reach point A. Then push your needle through to the wrong side of the appliqué and take an anchor stitch in the turn-under allowance. Run a row of small running stitches in the turn-under allowance only to point B and tighten the thread slightly. Finger press the area for the next stitches. Take an anchor stitch and another row of running stitches back to point A (Fig. 2–14). Tighten the thread slightly if necessary, then take an anchor stitch and continue to appliqué-stitch area A-B.

Acute Angles

Clip acute angles to the fold, apply a fray inhibitor, and taper the allowance toward the angle. It's a good idea to put a second stitch in the point of the V. The stitching will be visible in this area, hence the importance of a well-matched thread. Place stitches so close together

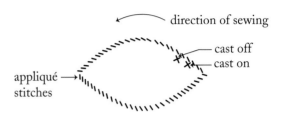

view from wrong side of background fabric

Fig. 2–12.

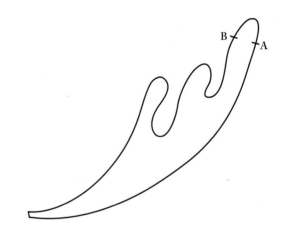

Fig. 2–13.

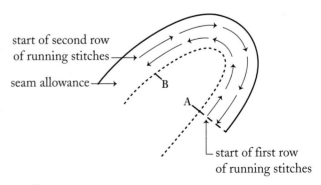

Fig. 2–14.

near the point that they almost resemble satin stitching. Visible stitches are better here than the possibility of fraying.

Sharp Points

There are two methods for handling sharp points that are equally effective. For the piece in

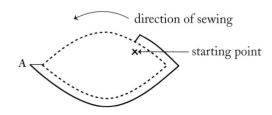

Fig. 2–15, stitch right up to point A and anchor the point with two stitches. Fold under the allowance beyond the point by pushing and stroking the allowance with a stout needle or pin. When all of the allowance is neatly tucked away, flatten the area with your fingers and continue to appliqué.

For the second method, when you are approaching point A, fold the fabric beyond the point toward you at first. Finger press the fold firmly. Then fold the fabric away from you. The allowance at the point will stay tucked under better with this method. Again, taking two stitches right in the point is beneficial.

Fig. 2–15.

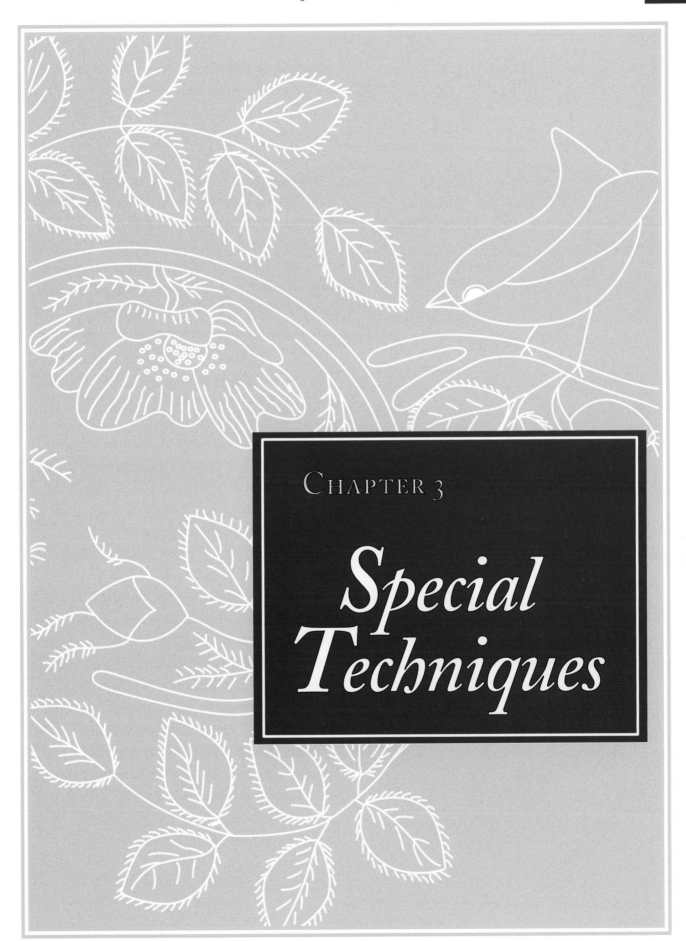

CHAPTER 3

Special Techniques

Margaret Docherty

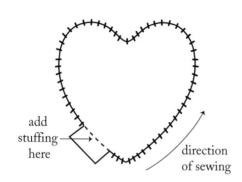

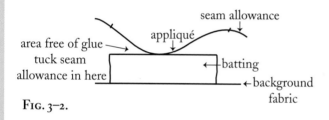

FIG. 3–1.

FIG. 3–2.

BLOCK 30, FANCY FRUIT BASKET

Stuffed Appliqué

With the small-scale appliqué, as found in Little Brown Bird, the best way to obtain a three-dimensional effect is by stuffing the individual flower petals with a quality, soft, toy stuffing. You can use an orange stick to insert the stuffing into the space between the background fabric and the motif after most of it has been appliquéd (Fig. 3–1). As in toy making, use enough stuffing to make the piece bulge and appear fat, then complete the appliqué stitches on the appliqué. Where one piece overlaps another, and for the center of a flower, be sure your appliqué stitches go through *all* layers, including the background fabric, and keep your stitches close together. You may have to resort to stab stitching in some thick areas.

After you finish each block, rinse it well to remove all traces of the markings on the background fabric and to remove the spray starch. Press the finished block while it is still damp, which settles the stuffing into a nicely raised layer with a "plateau" rather than a "mole-hill" effect.

As an alternative way of stuffing, and one that is more suitable for large areas, cut a piece of batting slightly smaller than the appliqué template. Position the batting on the background fabric and appliqué over it. You may find it easier to sew if you attach the batting to the wrong side of the appliqué piece with a little basting glue. Keeping the batting within the stitching lines, leave the edges of the batting free of glue so there is room to tuck in the turn-under allowance (Fig. 3–2). This method was used to pad Fancy Fruit Basket (Block 30).

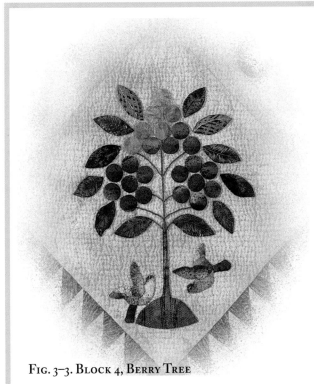

FIG. 3–3. BLOCK 4, BERRY TREE

BERRIES

There are three different types of berries in the quilt: unstuffed, slightly stuffed, and heavily stuffed (Fig. 3–3). Because the berries are so small, you will need accurate templates, which you can make from fine cardboard, such as found in old greetings cards.

Unstuffed berries. If you want a perfect circle, you need to use an accurate master template. At office-supply stores, you can buy a commercial plastic template that contains various sizes of circular holes. For greatest accuracy, use the commercial template to draw circles the sizes needed on cardboard. Then cut out the circles accurately and make sure the edges are smooth. If your cardboard template has jagged edges, the irregularities will appear in your finished appliqué. Use an emery board, if necessary, to smooth the edges of the template.

Alternatively, you may not want your berries to be perfect circles. You can just draw round

shapes free-hand on cardboard for a more natural effect. Again, take care to keep the edges smooth when you cut the templates.

To find what size circle to cut for a specific berry, decide on the diameter of the berry you want to make. Add at least ¼" for a turn-under allowance all around. For example, if you want a ½" berry, add ½" (2 x ¼") for seam allowances, which equals a 1" circle. To allow a little margin for error, you may want to add another ⅛". Therefore, you would draw and cut fabric circles that are 1⅛" in diameter to finish with a berry ½" in diameter. Excess fabric can be trimmed away as you sew. Lightly starch your fabric before cutting.

To turn under the allowance on such a small circle, you can use a dressmaker's technique for gathering: Sew a line of small running stitches around the edge of the fabric circle. Draw the threads up slightly and insert your cardboard template. You can use just one row of gathering stitches to make a berry, but you will get a smoother effect if you use two rows of stitches. Place the second stitching line as close to the edge of the template as possible but make sure it is still within the seam allowance. Pull the threads tight. The fabric will take on the shape of the template with the allowance gathered up on the wrong side of the berry (Fig. 3–4). Tie off the thread.

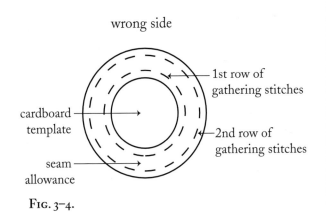

wrong side

1st row of gathering stitches

cardboard template

2nd row of gathering stitches

seam allowance

FIG. 3–4.

Block 23, Crown of Oak

Press the finished gathered circle with the template still in place. For very small circles where it is obviously going to be tricky to remove the template, starch the circle well and press for a second time.

The circle is ready to be appliquéd to the background fabric. Here are two ways for doing this:

1. Leave the template in place. Trim the seam allowance neatly. Stitch the circle to the background and admire your perfect result. Make a small cross-shaped incision in the background fabric behind the appliquéd circle. Through this hole, remove the cardboard template by using a stout needle to lift a section of it and a pair of fine-pointed tweezers to pull it out (Fig. 3–5).

This method gives a beautiful result, but it is not really feasible for very small berries. Be wary of using this method for areas where there is a high density of berries. Your background fabric will be pierced with multiple cuts, which could fray over a period of years of washing and use.

2. Remove the template before appliquéing the circle to the background fabric. Trim the turn-under allowance and use a stout needle and fine-pointed tweezers to remove the cardboard. You may need to nip a stitch in both gathering rows to do this. If you have starched your fabric well, the circular shape should hold, and the piece will appliqué neatly in place.

Slightly stuffed berries. Prepare a circle of fabric over a cardboard template as for unstuffed berries. Starch the fabric well and remove the

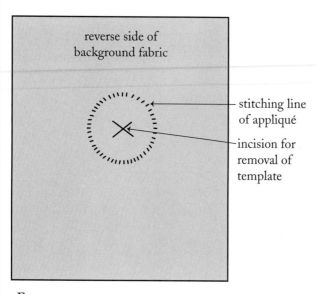

reverse side of background fabric

stitching line of appliqué

incision for removal of template

Fig. 3–5.

template. Appliqué the berry to the background fabric and fill with toy stuffing when approximately three-fourths of the appliqué stitches are in place. The berry should be well stuffed and bulging in the middle. Finish appliquéing the remainder of the berry to the background fabric (Fig. 3–6).

If you are concerned that adding stuffing will distort the shape of your berry, draw an accurate duplicate of the circle with a washable or erasable pen or pencil on your background fabric and make sure your appliqué stitches lie on this line (Fig. 3–7).

Rinse the completed appliqué block and press it while it is still damp. This method flattens the stuffing somewhat, leaving a nicely raised berry that does not resemble a mini molehill (Fig. 3–8).

Heavily stuffed berries. These are the most fun to do. They do not take a great deal of skill, and novices and non-quilters seem to notice them first, demanding "How did you do that?"

No cardboard templates are needed. Cut circles of lightly starched fabric approximately twice the size of the required finished berry.

Run a line of gathering stitches around the edge of the fabric circle and draw them up slightly to form a pouch. Rest the pouch on a firm surface and stuff very firmly with a toy stuffing. Use a firm, blunt object, such as the blunt end of a wooden kebab skewer, to push the stuffing hard into the fabric pouch. Pull your gathering stitches tight and look at the berry with a critical eye. The top side should be ball-shaped with no creases around its edges (Fig. 3–9).

If you are not satisfied with the result,

stuff here

FIG. 3–6.

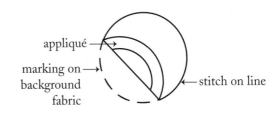

appliqué

marking on background fabric

stitch on line

FIG. 3–7.

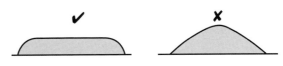

FIG. 3–8.

side view

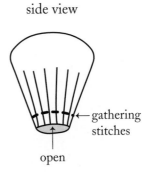

gathering stitches

open

FIG. 3–9.

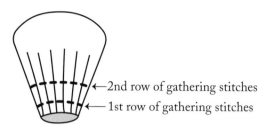

FIG. 3–10.

2nd row of gathering stitches
1st row of gathering stitches

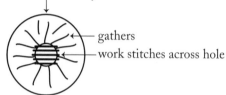

underside of berry

gathers
work stitches across hole

FIG. 3–11.

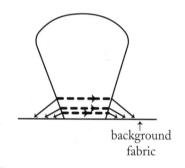

background fabric

FIG. 3–12.

release your gathering stitches and add more stuffing. When you are satisfied with the result, run a second row of gathering stitches around the circle nearer to the top surface (Fig. 3–10).

Take two or three small stitches to secure the gathering and, with the same thread, work large stitches across the opening of the pouch. This technique will keep the stuffing in place and, to some extent, will strengthen the raw edges of your fabric (Fig. 3–11).

Again take two or three small stitches to secure the thread. The prepared berry can be put aside until you are ready to appliqué, or you can continue with the same thread and immediately stitch the berry to the background fabric. Start by attaching the center of the berry, near the stuffing hole, and work round and round, taking stitches farther up the berry until you feel it is very firmly attached and all the raw edges and gathering stitches are hidden (Fig. 3–12). Tie a secure knot on the wrong side within the stitching line.

Fabric Painting

Fabrics can be painted with dyes or with special fabric paints, and there are a great variety of products available on the market. The cyclamen leaves in Block 39 were painted with acrylic paints (Fig. 3–13). Remember that fabric impregnated with these paints becomes quite thick and stiff. You will not need spray starch, and you may find the fabric difficult to manipulate for appliqué. Dye-painting is more specialized (see Bibliography, page 142), but the finished effect is less problematic for appliqué.

You can draw shapes in pencil on a well-washed white cotton fabric and paint them. When the paint is not quite dry, you can add blotches of other colors along the inside of the

FIG. 3–13. BLOCK 39, POT OF CYCLAMEN

pencil lines. When totally dry, the paints can be set with a hot iron. Wash the fabric in a couple of days just to be sure that the paint is colorfast. You can then cut the shapes out and appliqué them without spray starch.

Broderie Perse

These motifs are cut from fabric and applied to a background. Rose buds, some small roses, as well as a few leaves, were use to obtain a realistic effect that would not have been possible by standard appliqué methods in such a small scale.

The traditional method for broderie perse involves stitching the raw edges of the appliqué piece to the background with a decorative buttonhole or blanket stitch. Instead, a standard appliqué method was used, and the raw edges were turned under before the piece was stitched to the background (Fig. 3–14a–d).

Bias Strips for Stems and Baskets

Stems and other narrow pieces can be made by machine sewing a bias tube and pressing it flat over a bias pressing bar. Bias bars of different widths can be purchased at quilting stores or from sewing-supply catalogs. Pieces prepared in this way are easy to appliqué.

The appliqué for LITTLE BROWN BIRD is on a very small scale. Some of the bias strips are only ⅛" or ³⁄₁₆" wide. If you decide to increase the size of the blocks from their original 8" to 12" or larger, it would be quite acceptable to use bias strips ¼" wide, which are much easier to prepare.

When cutting and machine stitching bias strips, you may want to make a batch large enough to suffice for the whole quilt. It's a good idea to cut all your strips at the same time because it can be difficult to return to a piece of bias-cut

a. Block 33, Leafy Cornucopia

b. Block 34, Wreath with Bird

c. Block 35, Victorian Love Birds

Fig. 3–14 – d. Block 36, Pot of Roses

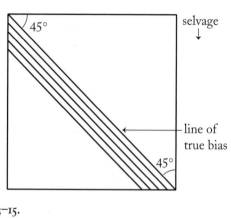

Fig. 3–15.

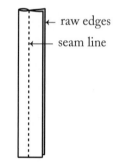

Fig. 3–16.

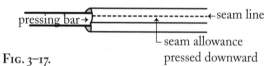

Fig. 3–17.

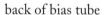

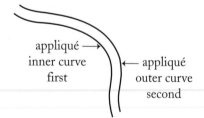

Fig. 3–18.

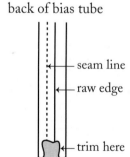

Fig. 3–19.

fabric to re-align it for further cutting. Starch your fabric well before cutting it. Cut on the true bias, that is, 45° to the selvage (Fig. 3–15).

With the fabric wrong sides together, finger press the bias strip so the raw edges meet neatly. Machine stitch down the whole length of the strip, using your ¼" presser foot, if you have one (Fig. 3–16).

Trim the seam allowance as close to the stitching line as you can manage. Insert a bias pressing bar into the tube, aligning the seam line near the center of the back side. With a hot iron, press (not iron) the seam allowances downward (Fig. 3–17). The seam allowances should not be visible on the front of the tube. If necessary, more spray starch can be applied to the seam allowances with a small paint brush.

Appliquéing Stems

Remember to stitch the inside of the curve first (Fig. 3–18). The bias cut will allow the outside of the curve to stretch to fit. If you stitch

---

How wide should a bias strip be?

Manufacturers of bias pressing bars give varying instructions for cutting fabric strips. The following formula can be used: Cut strips twice the finished width of the tube plus seam allowances.

For example: For a ⅛" finished bias tube, cut strip ¾" wide.

⅛" bias	cut ¾"
3/16" bias	cut 7⁄8"
¼" bias	cut 1"
⅜" bias	cut 1¼"

the outside curve first, you may get puckering when you stitch the inside curve. To stitch the raw ends of the bias tube under, trim the wrong side of the tube, particularly the seam allowance, to eliminate bulk (Fig. 3–19).

APPLIQUÉING WOVEN BASKETS

To avoid bulk on small blocks with many appliqué pieces, the bias tubes for the baskets were appliquéd directly to the background fabric instead of a foundation. If you use this method, be careful to keep your weaving close together to avoid having the background fabric show (Figs. 3–20a–g).

To ensure that the basket is stable, use a closely matched cotton thread and sew the ribs and weavers to the background fabric at their junctions.

★ = *stitch ends to background fabric.*

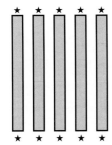

a. Odd number of ribs needed for basket to be symmetrical.

b. Weave over and under ribs.

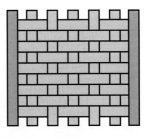

c. Alternate rows.

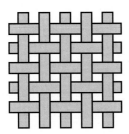

d. Continue weaving until the whole area is covered.

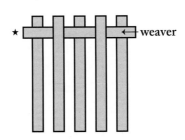

e. Push the weavers together so no background fabric is visible.

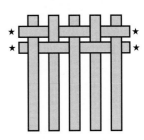

f. Appliqué side ribs to weaving to cover raw edges of weavers.

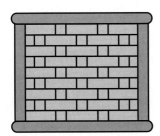

g. Appliqué top and bottom of basket to cover raw edges of ribs.

FIG. 3–20 a–g.

FIG. 3–21. BLOCK 19, PANSY BASKET

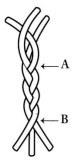

Secure plaited cord at points A & B with stitches in a closely matching thread.

FIG. 3–22.

FIG. 3–23. BLOCK 30, FANCY FRUIT BASKET

For a more decorative effect, the basket base and handle can be constructed from three pieces of bias tubing plaited together (Fig. 3–21).

In Block 30 (Fancy Fruit Basket), stuffed appliqué was combined with regular appliqué and broderie perse for the contents of the basket. The inspiration for the basket itself came from a greeting card depicting an embroidered basket. To achieve the desired effect, wadding was used as stuffing for the top of the basket and plaited cord for the body. The cords were twisted for the handle, and some loose cord was woven around the padded top of the basket. The cords were obtained from a spare length of upholstery braid. Once a cord was plaited, it was applied in much the same way as a bias strip, but each end was secured by stitching the cords together with a well-matched cotton thread (Fig. 3–22).

The loose cords trailing over the top of the basket are firmly anchored to the background fabric at all junctions with the rim of the basket (Fig. 3–23).

Embellishment

Simple embroidery and a permanent marker pen can transform a block from ordinary to quite realistic.

A lot of embroidery in a variety of threads was used to delineate the details on LITTLE BROWN BIRD, such as the fine stems, tendrils, ferns, flower centers, and the details on the birds. Stitches included French and bullion knots; stem and outline stitches; satin and textured satin stitches; and straight, chain, and daisy stitches (Fig. 3–24).

The majority of details, such as the ferns, rose centers, and the fine stems in the borders, were done with a very fine machine embroidery

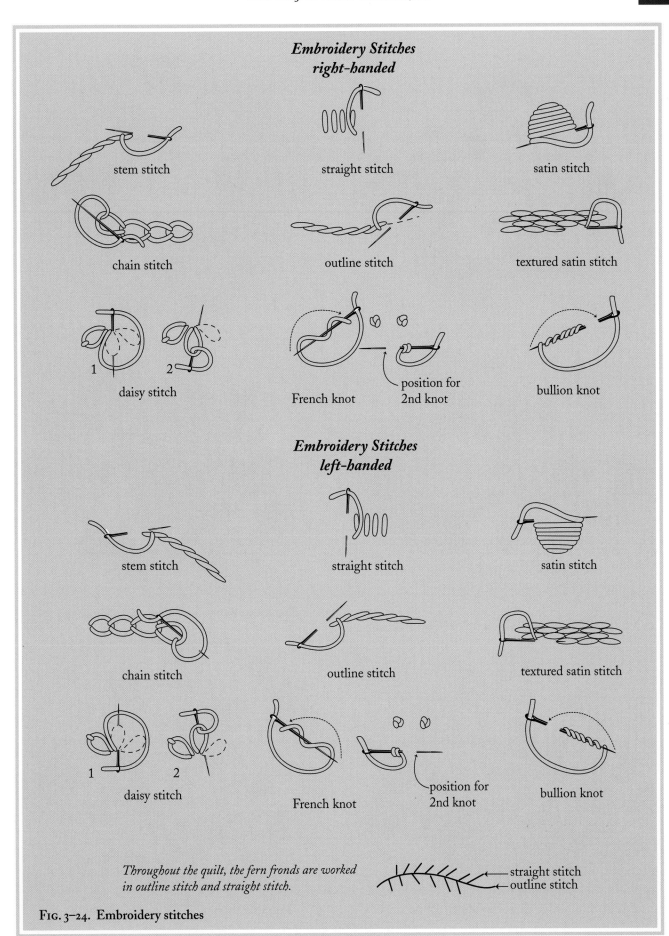

**Embroidery Stitches
right-handed**

stem stitch

straight stitch

satin stitch

chain stitch

outline stitch

textured satin stitch

1   2

daisy stitch

French knot

position for
2nd knot

bullion knot

**Embroidery Stitches
left-handed**

stem stitch

straight stitch

satin stitch

chain stitch

outline stitch

textured satin stitch

1   2

daisy stitch

French knot

position for
2nd knot

bullion knot

*Throughout the quilt, the fern fronds are worked
in outline stitch and straight stitch.*

straight stitch
outline stitch

FIG. 3–24. Embroidery stitches

FIG. 3–25a. BLOCK 2, BASKET OF POPPIES

FIG. 3–25d. BLOCK 38, CYCLAMEN WREATH

FIG. 3–25b. BLOCK 6, ROSE BASKET

FIG. 3–26. BLOCK 22, BOWL OF ANEMONIES

FIG. 3–25c. BLOCK 20, PANSY POSEY

FIG. 3–27. BLOCK 33, LEAFY CORNUCOPIA

or silk thread (Figs. 3–25a–d). Some stems were outlined with a single strand of embroidery thread, as were the centers of the anemones (Fig. 3–26).

A crochet cotton in variegated shades of brown was used for most of the tendrils and the seed heads in Block 33, the cornucopia of roses and blue bells (Fig. 3–27).

A shiny rayon thread was used to depict seed heads in Block 20, the bunch of pansies tied with red ribbon (Fig. 3–25c).

The small scale of the appliqué made even the finest embroidery line appear heavy in some instances. For these, size 01 permanent pens in black, brown, and green were used. Examples of pen embellishment include the veins of leaves and the fine hairs on the outer edges of some of the leaves. Sometimes, fine dots were added to the leaf fabric to enhance the texture (Fig. 3–28).

A pen was also used for some of the flowers. The roses in particular were totally transformed in appearance when fine veins were added to the petals with a brown pen (Fig. 3–29). The broderie perse buds were enhanced with "tufts" done with a size 01 brown pen (Fig. 3–30). For the rose hips, which were already stuffed, it was difficult to obtain a perfect shape for the finished berry. The inking with a black pen not only added a touch of realism but helped to camouflage imperfections in the shape (Fig. 3–31). In Blocks 6 (roses, Fig. 3–25b) and 19 (pansies), the flowers are set on a piece of green fabric, which was transformed into a mossy appearance simply by adding fine dots with a pen (Fig. 3–32, page 38).

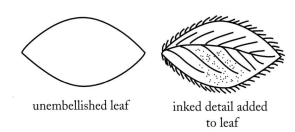

unembellished leaf · inked detail added to leaf

FIG. 3–28.

unembellished rose · rose with inked veins on petals, French knots in center, and embroidered stamens

FIG. 3–29.

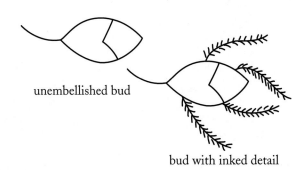

unembellished bud

bud with inked detail

FIG. 3–30.

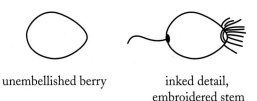

unembellished berry · inked detail, embroidered stem

FIG. 3–31.

FIG. 3–32. BLOCK 19, PANSY BASKET; BLOCK 20, PANSY
POSEY ; BLOCK 21, SHADES OF BLUE; BLOCK 22, BOWL
OF ANEMONIES

Chapter 4

Design

To design blocks like those in Little Brown Bird, complete with embellishing details, may appear at first glance to be rather intimidating. But anyone, even someone without drawing skills, can design such a block. If you would like to try your hand at designing your own blocks, the following tips may be helpful.

There are 15 wreaths in Little Brown Bird, and all originate from only three basic shapes (Fig. 4–1).

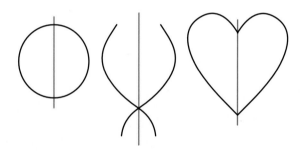

Fig. 4–1.

Fig. 4–2. Block 9, Heart Wreath

For each wreath, you can use two views of one large flower, a front view and a profile.

Add buds and smaller flowers or berries to fill in the gaps.

Flowers can be drawn free-hand or copied from other sources. (Be careful of copyrights, though.)

Once you have drawn your flowers, make several paper copies and cut them out.

Block 9 (Fig. 4–2) contains the same flowers on the same heart shape that were used for the heart design in Figs. 4–3 through 4–6, but the different positioning of the flowers creates a completely different wreath.

Step 1. Copy the heart pattern onto a piece of paper the size of the finished block.

Working on only the center and one side of the design, place your cut-out flowers around the basic shape until you find an arrangement that you like. Attach the paper flowers lightly with glue or draw around them (Fig. 4–3).

Step 2. Fill in the details, such as the leaves (Fig. 4–4).

Step 3. Add some details to be embroidered or drawn with ink to give an idea of how the finished block can look. Erase any unwanted lines, including the heart shape (Fig. 4–5). Inking and embroidery details do not need to be transferred to the background fabric.

Step 4. Complete the drawing of the whole block, paying particular attention to the leaves around the bottom center flower, because the design is not symmetrical (Fig. 4–6).

FIG. 4–3. Step 1

FIG. 4–5. Step 3

FIG. 4–4. Step 2

FIG. 4–6. Step 4

Margaret Docherty

CHAPTER 5

Quilt Instructions & Patterns

LITTLE BROWN BIRD *Pattern*
88" x 88"
Appliqué blocks 8" (finished)

YARDAGE AND CUTTING INSTRUCTIONS
(based on 44"-wide fabric)

Fabric	Yards	Meters
CREAM	8	7.2

40 blocks: cut 9" squares (a)

8 side triangles: cut four 9" squares in half (b)

4 corner triangles: cut one 9¼" square in quarters (c)

36 sashing strips, 2½" x 14½"

*4 border strips, 10" x 88"

Sawtooth sashing:

    266 squares, 1⅞", cut in half (d)

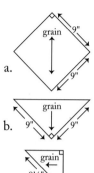

BLUE	2¾	2.5

*4 border strips, 1" x 72"

*4 border strips, 1" x 89"

36 sashing strips, 1" x 9½"

Bias binding strips, 1⅞" wide, 370" in length

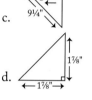

BROWN	2¾	2.5

*4 border strips, 1" x 71"

*4 border strips, 1" x 90"

36 sashing strips, 1" x 10½"

Sawtooth sashing

276 squares, 1⅞", cut in half (d)

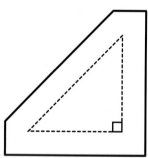

full-size d patch

BROWN	½	0.5

Stems for blocks and borders

PINK Roses	Fat quarters of five different values
YELLOW Roses	Fat quarters of five different values
GREEN Leaves	½ yard (0.5 meters) main fabric Fat quarters of 10 or 12 different fabrics
RED Berries	Fat quarters of **2** different fabrics

Fabric	Yards	Meters
AUTUMN PRINT	**FAT QUARTER**	

Scherenschnitte for Blocks 13, 14, 27, and 28

Scraps of other fabrics needed will be described in the pattern section.

BACKING	8¼	7.5
BATTING	92" x 92"	

Cutting instructions include ¼" seam allowances, except for appliquéd blocks and the appliquéd border, which could be distorted. Wider seam allowances have been added for these pieces.

*Measurements for borders include extra length for custom fitting to your quilt's actual measurements.

The dimensions of the quilt
(without seam allowances)

❧ ❧ ❧

Finished quilt, without binding, 88" x 88".

Appliqué blocks, 8" squares.

Blue and brown sashings, ½" wide.

Cream sashings, 2" wide.

Sawtooth sashings, 1" wide.

Inner, narrow brown border, 68" long on its inner side and ½" wide.

The inner narrow blue border measures 69" long on its inner side and ½" wide.

The appliqué border measures 70" long on its inner side and 8" wide. It measures 86" long on its outer side.

The outer blue border measures 86" long on its inner side and ½" wide.

The outer brown border measures 87" long on its inner side and is ½" wide.

Instructions for all blocks
* ❖ Refer to photo for fabric placement.
* ❖ Refer to Chapter 2, Neat & Tidy Appliqué, page 17.
* ❖ Refer to Chapter 3, Special Techniques, page 25, for block construction.
* ❖ Each pattern should be centered over a 9" block set diagonally.

Instructions for individual blocks include:
* ❖ Fabric not allowed for in LITTLE BROWN BIRD pattern.
* ❖ Special techniques used, including embellishment.
* ❖ Each pattern will show in at least one detail of inking or fine embroidery.

BLOCK 1: POTTED PLANT

Fabrics   ### *Placement*

Orange, red, yellow, pink	berries & flower
Blue	birds
Brown	tub, soil, tree stem
Fawn	tub
Yellow	bands on tub
Green	leaves

Special Techniques

FLAT BERRIES	scatter over leaves & in spaces (size is optional)

Embellishment

FABRIC PEN

Brown or green	leaf veins, stamens on flowers, birds' eyes
Black	detail on berries

EMBROIDERY

Fawn/brown	outline stitch top edge of tub
Green	outline stitch tendrils
Yellow	satin stitch bird's beak

sample embellished leaf

Little Brown Bird Patterns Block 1: Potted Plant

Margaret Docherty

BLOCK 2: BASKET OF POPPIES

Fabrics

	Placement
Basket weave pattern (5" x 5")	basket
Orange, pink, yellow, red	poppies & buds
Blue	three small flowers
Green bias tube	poppy stems
Green	leaves

Special Techniques

STUFFED APPLIQUÉ	stuff the poppy petals marked S

Embellishment

FABRIC PEN

Brown or green	leaf veins
Black	petal veins on poppies, markings on buds
Blue	petal veins on blue flowers

EMBROIDERY

Yellow	satin stitch centers of three blue flowers
Black	straight stitch, satin stitch, French knots at center of poppies
Green	stem stitch fine stems
	textured satin stitch for poppy bud stems
	satin stitch, calyxes of poppies

sample embellished flower

Little Brown Bird Patterns **Block 2**: Basket of Poppies

Margaret Docherty

Block 3: Floral Urn

Fabrics	*Placement*
Marbled or tie-dye fabric (6" x 6")	urn
Yellow	berries, centers of flowers
Yellow	berries, centers of flowers
Green	leaves

Special Techniques

Stuffed appliqué	stuff all flower petals
	slightly stuff berries (Type 2, pages 28–29)

Embellishment

Fabric pen

Brown or green	leaf veins
Brown	flower veins

Embroidery

Brown	stem stitch fine stems
	French knots for details around berries
Black or yellow	straight stitch; French knots for flower stamens

Margaret Docherty

sample
embellished
flower

LITTLE BROWN BIRD PATTERNS **BLOCK 3**: FLORAL URN

Margaret Docherty

Block 4: Berry Tree

This simple block, good for beginners, was inspired by a motif on a British School of Needlework tapestry that my mother almost completed before her death in 1986. Completed by me very amateurishly in 1987.

Fabrics *Placement*

    Pink, red, orange   berries

    Brown   tree trunk

    Green and brown   leaves

Special Techniques

    Flat berries

Embellishment

    Fabric Pen

        Brown or green   leaf veins

    Embroidery

        Brown   stem stitch fine stems

                textured satin stitch for main stem above trunk

Two small birds in green (see Block 1, page 47) were added to this block in the original quilt.

Little Brown Bird Patterns **Block 4: Berry Tree**

Margaret Docherty

Block 5: Rose Wreath

Fabrics	*Placement*
Red	buds
Green	buds
(⅛" x 16")	bias stem for roses
Yellow, pink	roses
Yellow, green, brown	rose centers and leaves

Special Techniques

Stuffed appliqué	stuff rose petals marked S
	slightly stuff berries (Type 2, pages 28–29)

Embellishment

Fabric Pen	
Brown or green	leaf veins, leaf hairs (see Block 7, page 59)
Brown	tufts on rosebuds (see Block 7, page 59)
	veins on petals
Black	details on rose hips
Embroidery	
Brown or green	stem stitch fine stems
Green	fern fronds
Green, brown or yellow	straight stitch and French knots
	or bullion knots for rose centers
	(cover the rose centers densely with knots)

sample
embellished
flower

LITTLE BROWN BIRD PATTERNS BLOCK 5: ROSE WREATH

Margaret Docherty

Block 6: Rose Basket

Fabrics	*Placement*
Brown	
(³⁄₁₆" x 64")	bias strips for basket
(¼" x 14")	bias strips for basket handles
Blue tie-dye (3" x 13")	ribbons
Moss green (2½" x 6½")	top of basket
Red	buds
Green	buds and leaves
(⅛" x 16")	bias stem for roses
Yellow, pink	roses
Yellow, green, brown	rose centers

Special Techniques

Stuffed Appliqué	stuff rose petals marked S
	slightly stuff berries (Type 2, pages 28–29)
Blue ribbon inset	basket

Embellishment

Fabric Pen

Brown or green	leaf veins, leaf hairs
Brown	tufts on rosebuds
	veins on petals
Black	details on rose hips

Embroidery

Brown or green	stem stitch fine stems
Green	fern fronds
Green, brown or yellow	straight stitch and French knots
	or bullion knots for rose centers
	(cover the rose centers densely with knots)

Margaret Docherty

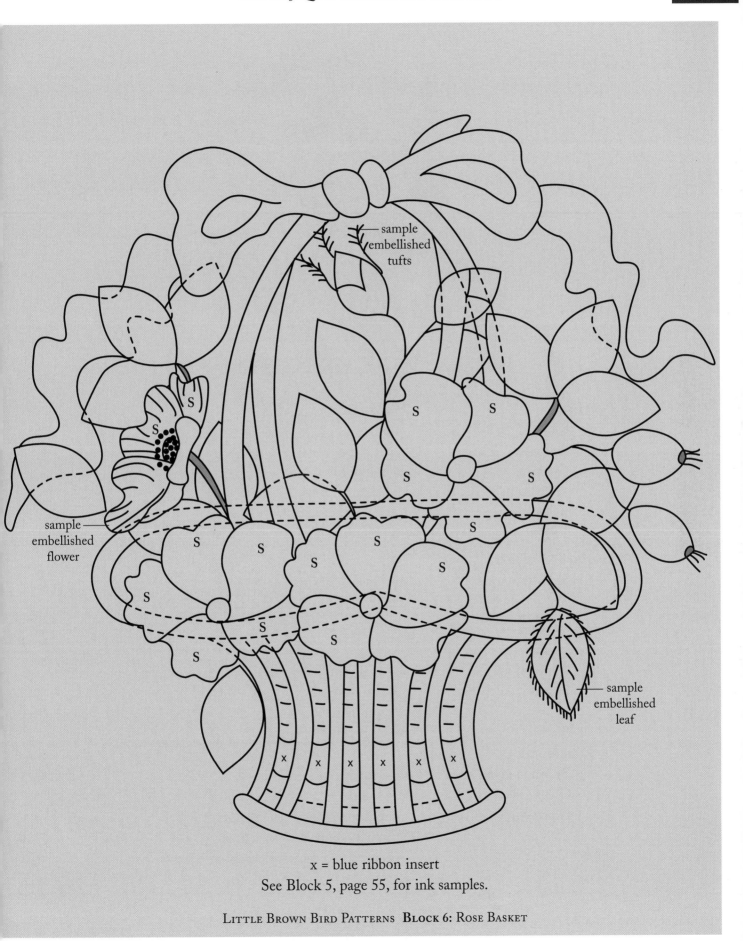

sample
embellished
tufts

sample
embellished
flower

sample
embellished
leaf

x = blue ribbon insert
See Block 5, page 55, for ink samples.

LITTLE BROWN BIRD PATTERNS **BLOCK 6: ROSE BASKET**

Margaret Docherty

BLOCK 7: VASE OF ROSES

Fabrics	*Placement*
Brown (5" x 2")	vase
Red	buds
Green	buds and leaves
(⅛" x 16")	bias stem for roses
yellow, pink	roses
Yellow, green, brown	rose centers

Special Techniques

STUFFED APPLIQUÉ	stuff rose petals marked S
	slightly stuff berries (Type 2, page 28–29)

Embellishment

FABRIC PEN

Brown or green	leaf veins, leaf hairs
Brown	tufts on rosebuds
	veins on petals
Black	details on rose hips

EMBROIDERY

Brown or green	stem stitch fine stems
Green	fern fronds
Green, brown or yellow	straight stitch and French knots
	or bullion knots for rose centers
	(cover the rose centers densely with knots)

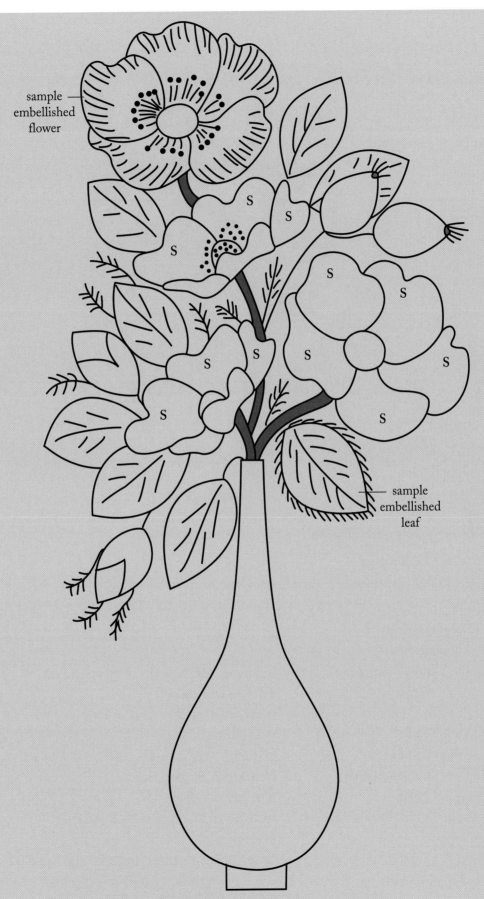

sample
embellished
flower

sample
embellished
leaf

Little Brown Bird Patterns Block 7: Vase of Roses

Margaret Docherty

BLOCK 8: ROSE SWIRL

Fabrics   *Placement*

Red	buds
Green	buds
(⅛" x 16")	bias stem for roses
yellow, pink	roses
Yellow, green, brown	rose centers and leaves

Special Techniques

STUFFED APPLIQUÉ	stuff rose petals marked S
	slightly stuff berries (Type 2, pages 28–29)

Embellishment

FABRIC PEN

Brown or green	leaf veins, leaf hairs
Brown	tufts on rosebuds
	veins on petals
Black	details on rose hips

EMBROIDERY

Brown or green	stem stitch fine stems
Green	fern fronds
Green, brown or yellow	straight stitch and French knots
	or bullion knots for rose centers
	(cover the rose centers densely with knots)

sample
embellished
flower

LITTLE BROWN BIRD PATTERNS BLOCK 8: ROSE SWIRL

Margaret Docherty

Block 9: Heart Wreath

Fabrics
Pink, purple (5" x 7")
Yellow
Purple
Green
(⅛" x 10")

Placement
flowers
berries
flower centers
calyxes and leaves
bias stems

Special Techniques
Stuffed appliqué

stuff all cosmos flower petals

stuff part of fuchsias marked S

slightly stuff berries (Type 2, pages 28–29)

Embellishment
Fabric pen
Green or brown   leaf veins
Brown   flower veins

Embroidery
Green

stem stitch fine stems of fuchsia, berries,
    and fern fronds

outline stitch tendrils around berries

satin stitch fuchsia calyxes

Deep pink or purple   stem stitch markings of fuchsia petals

stem stitch, French knots for fuchsia stamens

Black or brown   straight stitch, French knots for cosmos stamens

sample
embellished
flower

LITTLE BROWN BIRD PATTERNS BLOCK 9: HEART WREATH

Margaret Docherty

Block 10: Bluebird Wreath

Fabrics

	Placement
Blue	bird
Pink, purple	flowers
Yellow	berries
Purple	flower centers
Green	leaves

Special Techniques

Stuffed appliqué   stuff all cosmos flower petals

slightly stuff berries (Type 2, pages 28–29)

stuff part of fuchsias marked S

Embellishment

Fabric pen

Green or brown	leaf veins
Brown	flower veins

Embroidery

Green	stem stitch fine stems of fuchsia, berries, and fern fronds
	outline stitch tendrils around berries
	satin stitch fuchsia calyxes
Deep pink or purple	stem stitch markings of fuchsia petals
	stem stitch, French knots for fuchsia stamens
Black or brown	straight stitch, French knots for cosmos stamens

sample
embellished
flower

sample
embellished
leaf

sample
embroidery

LITTLE BROWN BIRD PATTERNS BLOCK 10: BLUEBIRD WREATH

Margaret Docherty

BLOCK 11: BLUE JUG

Fabrics

Blue (5" x 7")	jug
Pink, purple	flowers
Yellow	berries
Purple	flower centers
Green	calyxes and leaves
(⅛" x 10")	bias stems

Placement

Special Techniques

STUFFED APPLIQUÉ	stuff all cosmos flower petals
	stuff part of fuchsias marked S
	slightly stuff berries (Type 2, pages 28–29)

Embellishment

FABRIC PEN

Green or brown	leaf veins
Brown	flower veins

EMBROIDERY

Green	stem stitch fine stems of fuchsia, berries, and fern fronds
	outline stitch tendrils around berries
	satin stitch fuchsia calyxes
Deep pink or purple	stem stitch markings of fuchsia petals
	stem stitch, French knots for fuchsia stamens
Black or brown	straight stitch, French knots for cosmos stamens

sample
embellished
flower —

sample —
embellished
leaf

LITTLE BROWN BIRD PATTERNS BLOCK 11: BLUE JUG

Margaret Docherty

Block 12. Cosmos Swirl

Fabrics	*Placement*
Pink, purple	flowers
Yellow	berries
Purple	flower centers
Green	calyxes and leaves
(⅛" x 24")	bias stems (or embroider)

Special Techniques

Stuffed appliqué	stuff all cosmos flower petals
	stuff part of fuchsias marked S
	slightly stuff berries (Type 2, pages 28–29)

Embellishment

Fabric pen

Green or brown	leaf veins
Brown	flower veins

Embroidery

Green	stem stitch fine stems of fuchsia, berries, and fern fronds
	outline stitch tendrils around berries
	satin stitch fuchsia calyxes
Deep pink or purple	stem stitch markings of fuchsia petals
	stem stitch, French knots for fuchsia stamens
Black or brown	straight stitch, French knots for cosmos stamens

As an alternative for swirling stems, outline stitch edges in dark green or brown. Fill in center portion with textured satin stitch in a lighter green.

Margaret Docherty

REPEAT PATTERN

—sample
embellished
leaf

LITTLE BROWN BIRD PATTERNS BLOCK 12: COSMOS SWIRL

Margaret Docherty

Block 13: Appliquéd Feather

A tribute to quiltmakers of the past, the all-time favorite feathered circle quilting design is worked in reverse appliqué.

Scatter three or four flowers from Block 37, Fantasy Bird 1, across the appliquéd feather and join them with swirling tendrils in a green outline stitch.

Fabrics
Pink
Autumn print

Placement
flowers
Scherenschnitte

Little Brown Bird Patterns Block 13: Appliquéd Feather

Margaret Docherty

BLOCK 14: IMITATION SCHERENSCHNITTE

This two-layer design is not the classic paper-cut Scherenschnitte. The first layer is a reverse appliqué used for the flowers in Block 26, Autumn Bouquet.

As in Block 13, scatter three or four small flowers over the design and add swirling tendrils.

Fabrics	*Placement*
Pink, yellow	flowers and reverse appliqué marked X on pattern
Autumn print	Scherenschnitte

B

X
X   X
X
X
A
A
X
X
X
X
X
B

X = reverse appliqué

Little Brown Bird Patterns Block 14: Imitation Scherenschnitte

Margaret Docherty

BLOCK 15: BLUE TIT WREATH

Fabrics

Red, orange	leaves
Brown	central twig
⅜" x 16"	bias stems
Blue, blue-green,	
yellow	bird

Placement

Special Techniques

None

Embellishment

FABRIC PEN

Brown or black	leaf markings
Black	bird's eye

EMBROIDERY

Brown	stem stitch fine stems
Yellow/brown	satin stitch bird's beak
	stem stitch bird's feet
	outline stitch tendrils

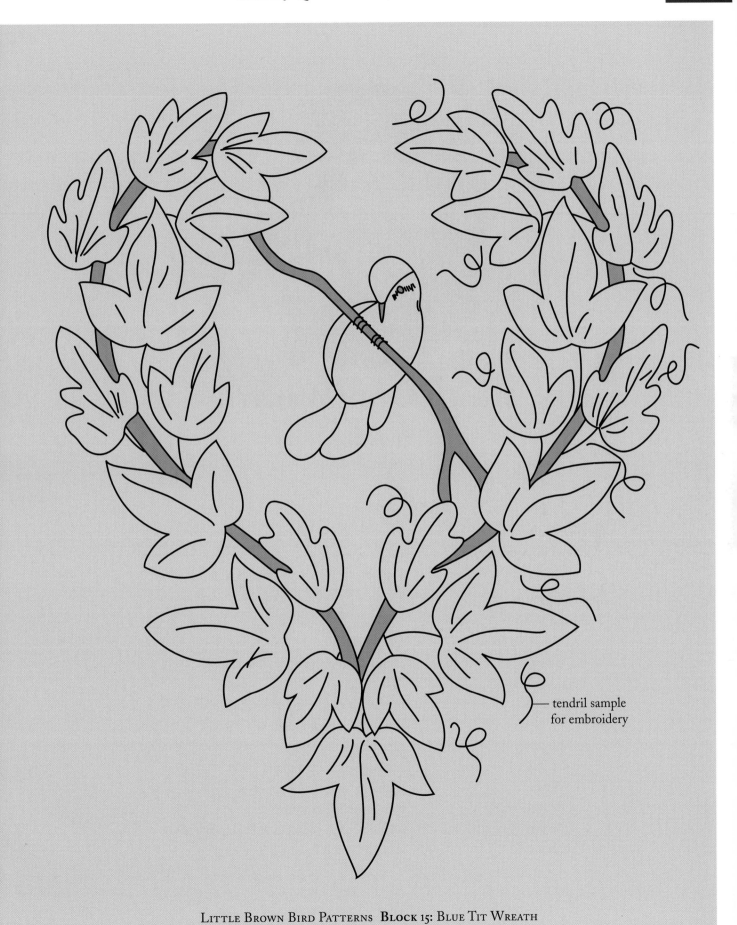

tendril sample
for embroidery

Little Brown Bird Patterns Block 15: Blue Tit Wreath

Margaret Docherty

Block 16: Open Wreath

Fabrics

    Brown

    Gray, brown

    Green

Special Techniques

    Stuffed appliqué

Embellishment

    Fabric pen

    Green or brown

    Black

    Embroidery

    Brown

    Black

    Yellow

    White

    Brown or green

    Brown

    Green

Placement

twig

bird

leaves

bird's wing

slightly stuff berries (Type 2, pages 28–29)

leaf veins

detail on rose hips

outline, straight stitch bird's legs

satin stitch bird's beak

satin stitch bird's eye

outline stitch bird's eye

highlight pupil of bird's eye

stem stitch fine stems

outline stitch center line on bird's tail

straight stitch hairs on leaves

sample
embroidery

sample
embellished
leaf

LITTLE BROWN BIRD PATTERNS BLOCK 16: OPEN WREATH

Margaret Docherty

Block 17: Little Brown Bird

Fabrics   *Placement*

Brown, fawn   central twig and bird
Pink   rose
Yellow   rose center
Green   leaves

Special Techniques

Stuffed Appliqué   stuff rose petals
                     slightly stuff berries (Type 2, pages 28–29)

Embellishment

Fabric Pen

Brown or green   leaf veins, leaf hairs
Brown   veins on petals
Black   details on rose hips

Embroidery

Brown   stem stitch fine stems
Yellow   straight stitch, French or bullion knots for
                        rose center (cover the rose center densely
                        with knots)
                     outline stitch bird's eye
Brown   outline, straight stitch bird's legs
                     satin stitch bird's beak
Black   satin stitch bird's eye

sample
embellished
leaf

Little Brown Bird Patterns Block 17: Little Brown Bird

Margaret Docherty

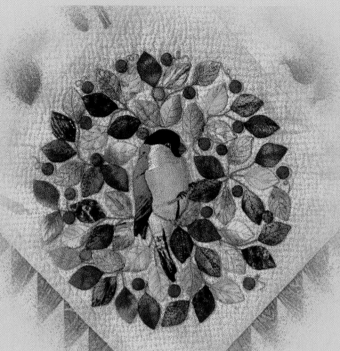

BLOCK 18: BULLFINCH RING

Fabrics

Pink	bird's breast
Black	bird's head
Black/gray	bird's wings and tail
Red	berries
Green and yellow	leaves

Special Techniques

STUFFED APPLIQUÉ — stuff bird's breast, wing, tail with pieces of batting

slightly stuff berries (Type 2, pages 28–29)

Embellishment

FABRIC PEN

Brown, green	leaf veins

EMBROIDERY

Brown or green	stem stitch fine stems
Brown	textured satin stitch for twig
Black	outline stitch bird's feet
	satin stitch bird's eye
White	highlight bird's eye
	straight stitch area A on pattern
Gray	satin stitch bird's beak
Brown	outline stitch tendrils

sample
embellished
leaf

tendril sample
for embroidery

A

Little Brown Bird Patterns Block 18: Bullfinch Ring

Margaret Docherty

Block 19: Pansy Basket

Fabrics	*Placement*
Blue, yellow, purple, maroon	pansies
Blue	small flowers
Moss green (2½" x 6½")	top of basket
Dark brown (³⁄₁₆" x 110")	bias tubing for basket
Green	leaves

Special Techniques

Stuffed appliqué	stuff pansy petals marked S
Woven Basket	plaited bias-strip base and handle
	(See Block 6, page 56, for pattern of the top of basket.)

Embellishment

Fabric pen

Brown or green	leaf veins
Black	stamens on small blue flowers
	dots on mossy green basket top

Embroidery

Green	stem stitch fine stems
Yellow	French knots for centers of small flowers
Black & yellow	satin stitch triangular centers of pansies
White, blue, red, black, yellow	straight stitch markings on pansy petals
Green	add fern fonds as desired

Margaret Docherty

LITTLE BROWN BIRD PATTERNS **BLOCK 19:** PANSY BASKET

Margaret Docherty

BLOCK 20: PANSY POSY

Fabrics

    Light red, dark red
    Yellow, purple, blue
    Green

Placement

ribbon
flowers
leaves

Special Techniques

STUFFED APPLIQUÉ   construct heart-shaped leaves in two sections,
                                stuff one half
                        stuff flower petals

Embellishment

FABRIC PEN

    Green or brown   leaf veins
    Black   center triangle of flowers
                                    (alternatively use black satin stitch)
                        some petal markings

Some heart-shaped leaves can be appliquéd as a single unit and the center line marked with a green or brown fabric pen.

EMBROIDERY

    Brown   stem stitch fine stems
    Yellow   straight stitch markings on petals
    Yellow and brown   daisy stitch seed heads
                                    (Use brown first; add yellow daisy stitch
                                    inside brown.)

Little Brown Bird Patterns **Block 20: Pansy Posy**

Margaret Docherty

Block 21: Shades of Blue

Fabrics	*Placement*
Terra cotta (8" x 3")	bowl
Blue, lilac	flowers
Yellow	flower centers
Green	leaves

Special Techniques

Stuffed appliqué   construct heart-shaped leaves in two sections, stuff one half

stuff flower centers

pad top and bottom of bowl with batting

Embellishment

Embroidery

Brown	stem stitch stems
Yellow	straight stitch, French knots for flower stamens
Green & yellow	add fern fronds as desired

Construct flowers from six identical circles. Circles for flower centers are smaller. Appliqué as for flat berries.

embroidery
sample

Little Brown Bird Patterns Block 21: Shades of Blue

Margaret Docherty

BLOCK 22: BOWL OF ANEMONES

Fabrics	*Placement*
Terra cotta (3" x 8")	bowl
Blue, red, purple	flowers
Black	flower centers
Green (⅛" x 8")	bias stems
	stem and calyx, marked C on pattern
Leafy fabric	broderie perse leaves

Special Techniques

STUFFED APPLIQUÉ	stuff all flower petals
BRODERIE PERSE	leaves

Embellishment

FABRIC PEN

Black	veins on petals

EMBROIDERY

Black	French knots or bullion knots for flower centers
	straight stitch, French knots for stamens
White	French or bullion knots for flower centers
Green	stem stitch fronds, marked F on pattern

Little Brown Bird Patterns Block 22: Bowl of Anemones

Margaret Docherty

BLOCK 23: CROWN OF OAK

Fabrics	*Placement*
Autumn shades	leaves
Pale yellow, olive or	
dark gray	acorns
Blue	bow
Red	berries
Brown (³⁄₁₆" x 16")	bias stem

Special Techniques

STUFFED APPLIQUÉ	slightly stuff red berries and top of acorns
	(Type 2, pages 28–29)

Embellishment

FABRIC PEN	
Brown	leaf veins
Black	details on acorns
EMBROIDERY	
Brown	stem stitch or textured satin stitch fine stems

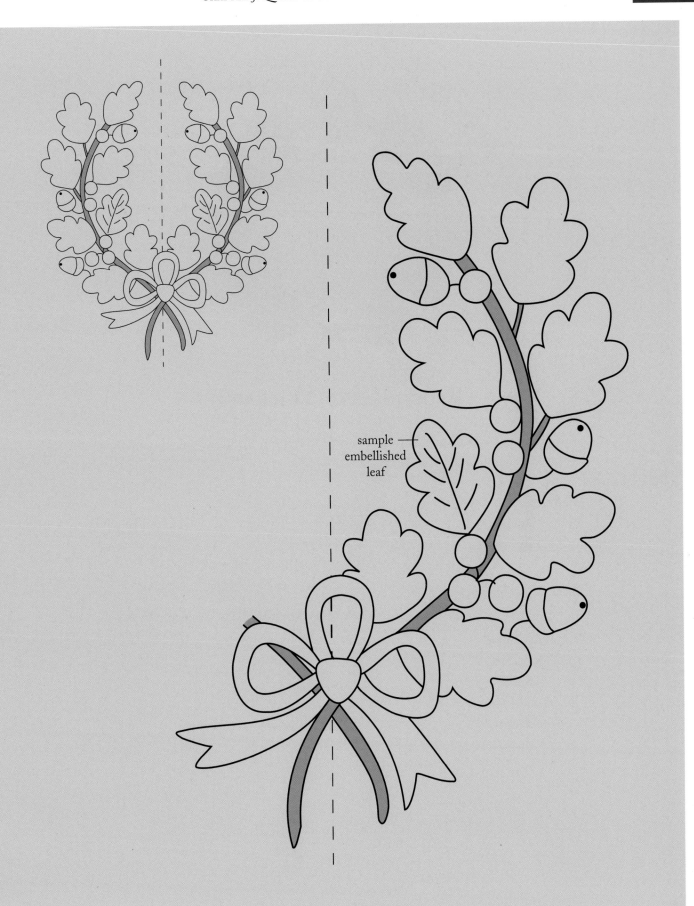

sample
embellished
leaf

LITTLE BROWN BIRD PATTERNS **BLOCK 23: CROWN OF OAK**

Margaret Docherty

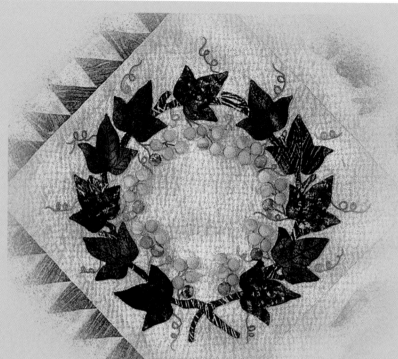

BLOCK 24: IVY WREATH

This block was inspired by the beautiful Baltimore Album Quilt Block known as Lovely Lane's Grapevine Wreath.

Fabrics	*Placement*
Yellows	berries
Brown	twig wreath
Green	leaves

Special Techniques

STUFFED APPLIQUÉ	slightly stuff berries (Type 2, pages 28–29)

Embellishment

FABRIC PEN

Black	leaf markings

EMBROIDERY

Brown	stem stitch fine stems of berries
Browns	outline stitch tendrils

sample
embellished
leaf

Little Brown Bird Patterns Block 24: Ivy Wreath

Margaret Docherty

BLOCK 25: CROWN OF IVY

Fabrics

Autumn shades	leaves
Red	berries
Blue tie-dye	bow
Brown (³⁄₁₆" x 12")	bias stem

Placement

Special Techniques

STUFFED APPLIQUÉ   slightly stuff berries (Type 2, pages 28–29)

Embellishment

FABRIC PEN

    Black   leaf markings

EMBROIDERY

    Brown   stem stitch fine stems of berries
    Browns   outline stitch tendrils

Margaret Docherty

sample
embellished
leaf

LITTLE BROWN BIRD PATTERNS BLOCK 25: CROWN OF IVY

Margaret Docherty

BLOCK 26: AUTUMN BOUQUET

Fabrics	*Placement*
Blue	bow
Dark brown or red	outer section of flowers
Pink or yellow	inner section of flowers are reverse appliqué, marked X on pattern
Green and yellow	leaves

Special Techniques   none

Embellishment

FABRIC PEN

Brown or green	leaf markings
Black	flower stamens

EMBROIDERY

Brown	stem stitch fine stems

— sample embellished stamens

X = reverse appliqué

Little Brown Bird Patterns Block 26: Autumn Bouquet

Margaret Docherty

BLOCK 27: SCHERENSCHNITTE 1

Fabrics	*Placement*
Pink, yellow	reverse appliqué, marked X on pattern
	small flowers
Autumn print	Scherenschnitte

Scatter small flowers from Block 37 across surface of pattern. Join flowers with embroidered swirling tendrils.

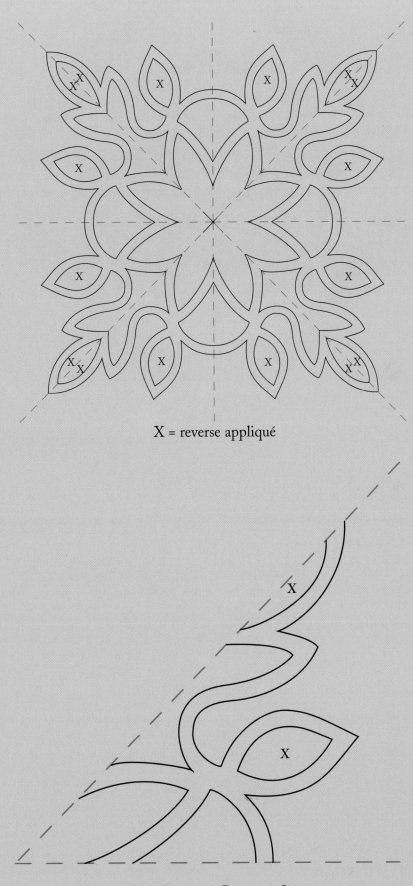

X = reverse appliqué

LITTLE BROWN BIRD PATTERNS **BLOCK 27:** SCHERENSCHNITTE 1

Margaret Docherty

BLOCK 28: SCHERENSCHNITTE 2

Fabrics	*Placement*
Pink, yellow	reverse appliqué, marked X on pattern
	small flowers
Autumn print	Scherenschnitte

Scatter small flowers from Block 37 across surface of pattern. Join flowers with swirling tendrils embroidered.

X = reverse appliqué

Margaret Docherty

BLOCK 29: STRAWBERRY WREATH

Fabrics

Placement

Red — strawberries (broderie perse was used in the original quilt)

Green — leaves

Special Techniques

STUFFED APPLIQUÉ — slightly stuff berries (Type 2, pages 28–29)

Embellishment

FABRIC PEN

Green or brown — leaf veins and hairs

EMBROIDERY

Green — stem stitch strawberry stems

White — French knots for berries

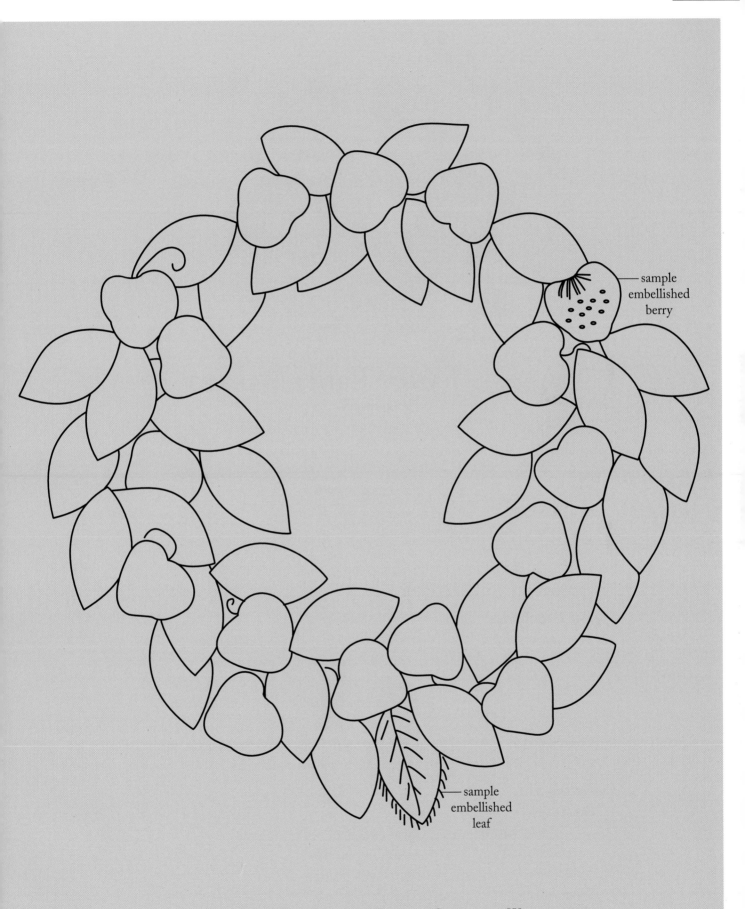

sample
embellished
berry

sample
embellished
leaf

LITTLE BROWN BIRD PATTERNS BLOCK 29: STRAWBERRY WREATH

Margaret Docherty

BLOCK 30: FANCY FRUIT BASKET

Fabrics

	Placement
Moss green (6" x 7")	basket top, brim and foundation of base
Yellow, red, purple, apple green	fruits (Some fruits in original quilt were broderie perse.)
Yellow and olive green or gray	acorns
Fawn, brown, or green cord (7 yds.)	basket
Green	leaves

Special Techniques

STUFFED APPLIQUÉ	brim of basket with piece of batting
	stuff the fruits as for flower petals
	slightly stuff rose hips (Type 2, pages 28–29)
	heavily stuff small berries to left of basket (Type 3, pages 29–30)
CORD BASKET	ribs, base strip (See photo for cord placement; handle is twisted cord.)

Embellishment

FABRIC PEN	
Green or brown	leaf markings
Black	markings on fruits
Brown	tufts on rose hips
EMBROIDERY	
Brown	stem stitch fine stems

Margaret Docherty

Little Brown Bird Patterns   Block 30: Fancy Fruit Basket

Margaret Docherty

BLOCK 31: CREANA'S FRUIT BASKET

This block was named after a friend who sketched it for me.

Fabrics
Basket weave (6" x 7")
Red, yellow, green
Green

Placement
basket
fruit
leaves

Special Techniques
STUFFED APPLIQUÉ   stuff fruits as for flower petals

Embellishment
FABRIC PEN
Green or brown   leaf markings
Brown or black   markings on fruits
EMBROIDERY
Brown   satin stitch fruit stems

LITTLE BROWN BIRD PATTERNS BLOCK 31: CREANA'S FRUIT BASKET

Margaret Docherty

Block 32: Crown of Strawberries

Fabrics	*Placement*
Red	strawberries (Broderie perse was used in the original quilt.)
Brown (³⁄₁₆" x 14")	bias stem
Green	leaves

Special Techniques

Stuffed appliqué	slightly stuff berries (Type 2, pages 28–29)

Embellishment

Fabric pen	
Green or brown	leaf veins and hairs
Embroidery	
Green	stem stitch strawberry stalks and calyx
	straight stitch hair on leaves (can be embroidered)
White	French knots for berries

sample
embellished
leaf

sample
embellished
berry

LITTLE BROWN BIRD PATTERNS BLOCK 32: CROWN OF STRAWBERRIES

Margaret Docherty

BLOCK 33: LEAFY CORNUCOPIA

If you use broderie perse flowers, which were used in the quilt, you will need 6 flowers in antique shades of pink and fawn.

Fabrics	*Placement*
Red	rose buds
Green	rose buds and leaves
Blue	bell flowers

Special Techniques
STUFFED APPLIQUÉ

    stuff roses
    stuff half of bluebell flowers

Embellishment
FABRIC PEN

Brown or green	leaf vein markings
Brown	tufts on rose buds and roses
	flower stamens, seed heads

EMBROIDERY

Brown & green	stem stitch, textured satin stitch fine stems
Yellow or brown	stem stitch, French knots for stamens of bluebells
Brown, fawn	French dots for seed heads
Yellows, greens	fill in liberally with fern fronds (not marked on pattern)

sample
embellished
tufts

sample
embellished
leaf

LITTLE BROWN BIRD PATTERNS BLOCK 33: LEAFY CORNUCOPIA

Margaret Docherty

BLOCK 34: WREATH WITH BIRD

If you use broderie perse flowers, which were used in the quilt, you will need 3 flowers in antique shades of pink and fawn.

Fabrics	*Placement*
Red	rose buds
Green	rose buds and leaves
Blue	bell flowers
Pink, gray, or black	bird
Yellow	berries

Special Techniques

STUFFED APPLIQUÉ	stuff roses
stuff half of bluebell flowers
slightly stuff yellow berries
(Type 2, pages 28–29)

Embellishment

PIGMA PEN

Brown or green	leaf vein markings
Brown	tufts on rose buds and roses
Black	bird's eye

EMBROIDERY

Brown, green	stem stitch, textured satin stitch for fine stems
Yellow or brown	stem stitch, French knots for stamens of bluebells
Brown	stem stitch, straight stitch birds' legs and feet
Brown or yellow	satin stitch birds' beak
outline stitch birds' eye

Margaret Docherty

sample embellished leaf

sample embellished leaf

sample embellished bud

LITTLE BROWN BIRD PATTERNS BLOCK 34: WREATH WITH BIRD

Margaret Docherty

Block 35: Victorian Love Birds

If you use broderie perse flowers, which were used in the quilt, you will need 5 flowers in antique shades of pink and fawn.

Fabrics

	Placement
Red	rose buds
Green	rose buds and leaves
Blue	bell flowers
Yellow, olive, or gray	acorns
Yellow, brown	acorn leaves
Brown	twigs
Browns, blue, pink	birds

Special Techniques

Stuffed appliqué	stuff roses
	optional – stuff wings of birds
	slightly stuff tops of acorns
	(Type 2, pages 28–29)

Embellishment

Fabric pen

Brown or green	leaf vein markings
Brown	tufts on rose buds and roses
Black	markings on acorns

Embroidery

Brown & green	stem stitch, textured satin stitch for fine stems
Brown	stem stitch, straight stitch birds' legs and feet
Black	satin stitch birds' eyes
White	highlight birds' eyes
	outline stitch wing and tail markings on birds
Brown or yellow	satin stitch birds' beaks
	outline stitch birds' eyes
Blue	stem stitch heart shape

sample
embellished
leaf

sample
embellished
leaf

sample
embellished
bud

LITTLE BROWN BIRD PATTERNS BLOCK 35: VICTORIAN LOVE BIRDS

Margaret Docherty

BLOCK 36: POT OF ROSES

Fabrics

Placement

If you use broderie perse flowers, which were used in the quilt, you will need 9 flowers in antique shades of pink and fawn.

Red	rose buds
Green	rose buds and leaves
Blue	bell flowers
Terra cotta (4½" x 7")	bowl
	optional – ornamental strip for top of bowl

Special Techniques

STUFFED APPLIQUÉ	stuff roses

Embellishment

FABRIC PEN

Brown or green	leaf vein markings
Brown	tufts on rose buds and roses

EMBROIDERY

Brown & green	stem stitch, textured satin stitch for fine stems
Yellow, green	fill in liberally with fern fronds
	(not marked on pattern)

sample
embellished
leaf

sample
embellished
bud

LITTLE BROWN BIRD PATTERNS **BLOCK 36: POT OF ROSES**

Margaret Docherty

BLOCK 37: FANTASY BIRD 1

Fabrics

Yellow (5"x6")	bird's body
Pink, yellow	flowers
Bright yellow	flower centers
Green	leaves

Special Techniques

STUFFED APPLIQUÉ	stuff flower petals individually

Embellishment

FABRIC PEN

Green or brown	leaf markings
Black	markings on petals
	stamens
	(alternatively, work in outline stitch and French knots)

EMBROIDERY

Brown	satin stitch bird's beak
White	satin stitch white of bird's eye and highlight in pupil
Black	satin stitch pupil of eye
Brown	outline stitch outline bird's eye

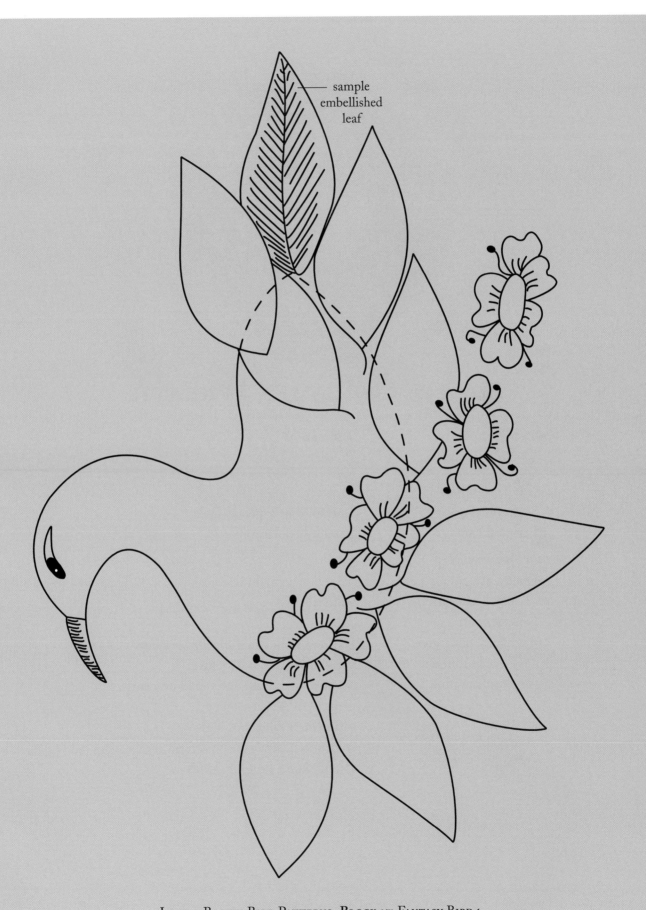

sample
embellished
leaf

LITTLE BROWN BIRD PATTERNS **BLOCK 37: FANTASY BIRD 1**

Margaret Docherty

Block 38: Cyclamen Wreath

Fabrics	*Placement*
Pink tie-dyes	flowers

Special Techniques

Stuffed appliqué	stuff all flower petals, buds
Painted Fabric	paint cyclamen leaves

Embellishment

Fabric pen

Black or brown	leaf veins

Embroidery

Mixed pink, green	textured satin stitch for flower stems
Green or brown	stem stitch fine leaf stems
Purple or pink	outline stitch buds and detail on center petal of flowers
Brown	satin stitch calyxes of buds
Green	stem stitch, straight stitch fern fronds
Pink	French knots on fern fronds

sample
embellished
leaf

LITTLE BROWN BIRD PATTERNS BLOCK 38: CYCLAMEN WREATH

Margaret Docherty

Block 39: Pot of Cyclamen

Fabrics

Pink tie-dyes

Terra cotta (4" x 4")

Placement

flowers

pot

Special Techniques

Stuffed appliqué

Painted Fabric

stuff all flower petals, bud

paint cyclamen leaves

Embellishment

Fabric pen

Black or brown

Embroidery

Mixed pink, green

Green or brown

Purple or pink

Brown

leaf veins

textured satin stitch for flower stems

stem stitch fine leaf stems

outline stitch buds and detail on center
petal of flowers

satin stitch calyxes of buds

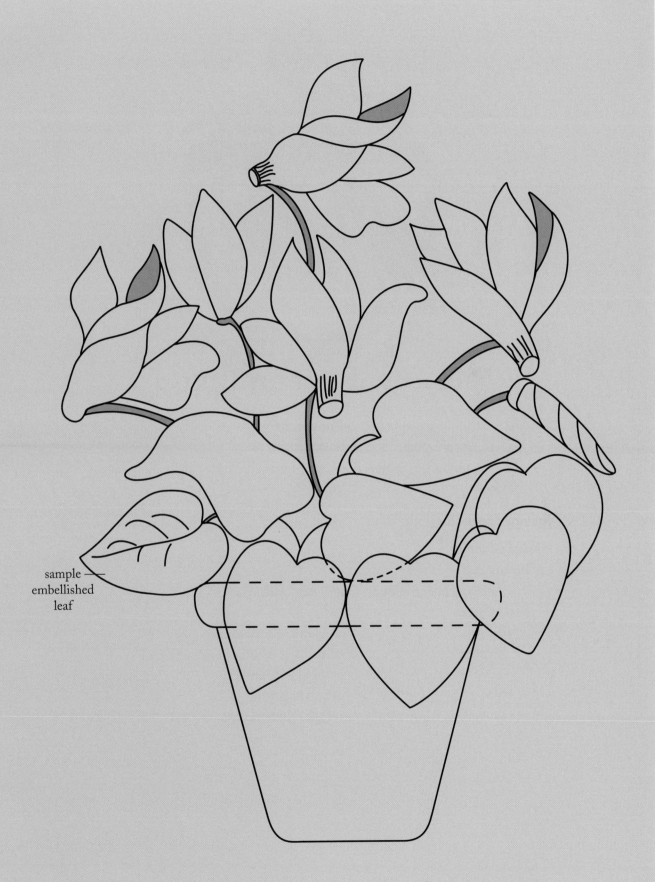

sample —
embellished
leaf

Little Brown Bird Patterns Block 39: Pot of Cyclamen

Margaret Docherty

BLOCK 40: FANTASY BIRD 2

Fabrics

Placement	

Fabrics · *Placement*

Red, purple, pink — bird feathers
Deep pink (3½" x 4½") — body of bird
Green — leaves

Special Techniques — none

Embellishment

FABRIC PEN

Black, green, or brown — leaf vein markings

EMBROIDERY

Browns — satin stitch bird's beak
White — satin stitch white of bird's eye and highlight in pupil
Black — satin stitch pupil of eye
Brown — outline stitch outline bird's eye

sample
embellished
leaf

LITTLE BROWN BIRD PATTERNS BLOCK 40: FANTASY BIRD 2

Margaret Docherty

SIDE TRIANGLE

(Make 8)

Fabrics   ***Placement***
  Yellow, pink   berries
  Brown   central top branch
  Green   leaves

Special Techniques
  STUFFED APPLIQUÉ   fully stuff berries (Type 3, pages 29–30)

Embellishment
  FABRIC PEN
  Black or brown   leaf markings
  EMBROIDERY
  Brown   stem stitch fine stems
  Brown, yellow   outline stitch tendrils

sample
embellished
leaf

LITTLE BROWN BIRD PATTERNS SIDE TRIANGLE

Margaret Docherty

Corner Triangle

(Make 2 and 2 reversed)

Fabrics	**Placement**
Red and green	rose buds
Green (4 x 4½")	bias stems
Green	leaves
Yellow, pink	rose
Brown	rose center

Special Techniques

Stuffed Appliqué	rose petals, marked S on pattern
	lightly stuff berries (Type 2, pages 28–29)

Embellishment

Fabric pen

Brown or green	leaf markings, hairs on rose leaves
Brown	petal veins, tufts on rosebuds
Black	markings on rose hips

Embroidery

Green	stem stitch fine stems
Brown	French knots for rose center
Green	optional – add fern fronds if desired

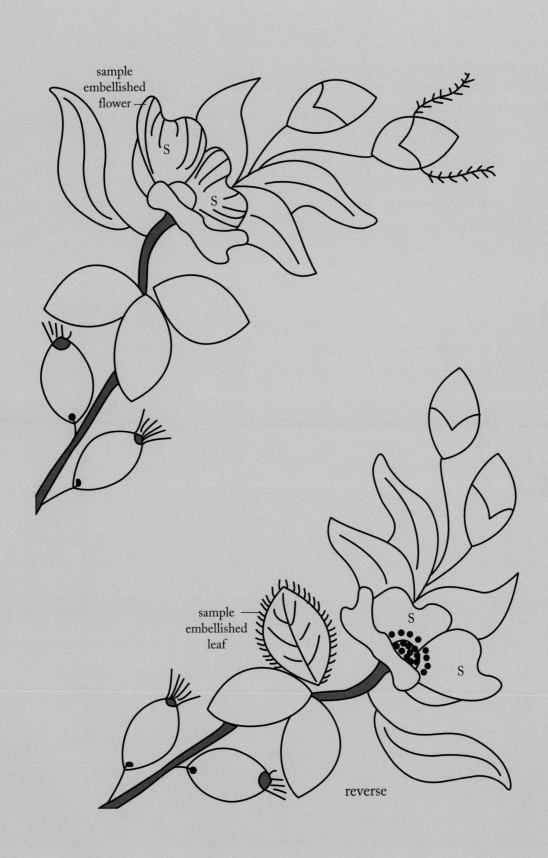

sample
embellished
flower

sample
embellished
leaf

reverse

LITTLE BROWN BIRD PATTERNS CORNER TRIANGLE

Margaret Docherty

APPLIQUÉD BORDER

Trace each border pattern as follows:

    Corner unit, A B A B A B A, center unit, Ar Br Ar Br Ar Br Ar, reverse corner unit. (To mark border for appliqué, center fabric on dashed pattern lines.)

Cut the following appliqué pieces:

- ❖ 32 yellow roses, unit A
- ❖ 24 pink roses, unit B
- ❖ 56 brown rose centers
- ❖ 56 rose buds
- ❖ 232 rose hips
- ❖ 56 (11½") brown bias stem, units A and B
- ❖ 8 (7½") brown bias stem, corner units
- ❖ 4 brown twigs, center units
- ❖ 852 rose leaves
- ❖ 48 ivy leaves, corner units
- ❖ 96 round red berries, corner units
- ❖ 4 brown birds, center units
- ❖ 4 blue bows, corner units

Fabrics	*Placement*
Yellow, pink tie-dyes	roses (use at least three values of one color for each rose)
Brown	bias stems, rose centers, twigs of center units, brown birds
Red, green	rose buds
Red, yellow	rose hips (at least two shades)
Autumn shades	ivy leaves
Red	round berries
Blue tie-dye	ribbons
Green, yellow, fawn, brown, orange red	rose leaves

Special Techniques

STUFFED APPLIQUÉ   stuff rose petals, marked S on unit B

lightly stuff rose hips (Type 2, pages 28–29)

fully stuff red berries in corner units
(Type 3, pages 29–30)

Embellishment

FABRIC PEN

Green or brown	leaf veins
Green or brown	hairs on rose leaves
Brown	tufts on rose buds
Brown	veins on rose petals
Black	markings on rose hips, red berries in corner units

Embroidery

Brown	French or bullion knots for rose centers
Brown	stem stitch fine stems of rose hips
Green or brown	stem stitch fine stems of rosebuds and leaves
	stem stitch stem in center unit
Dark green	textured satin stitch for leaf stems, ivy leaf stems in corner units
Greens	fern fronds in units A and B, marked E in unit B pattern

When each border appliqué is complete (apart from bow and stem which cross the seam area in the corner unit), rinse with water to remove markings on background fabric and press.

Measure the quilt for the border length. Because of the heavy stuffed appliqué and embroidery, which cause the background fabric to draw in, the borders were cut extra long and wide. Be sure to trim the borders equally at each end and on both sides to reach the desired measurements of 8½" x 86½". The finished border measurements are 70" for the inner edge, 86" for the outer edge, and 8" in width.

Join the appliquéd borders to the quilt (see Chapter 6 on quilt assembly). The last pieces of the corner appliqué unit can be stitched in place after all the borders are attached and mitered.

center unit

yellow rose

LITTLE BROWN BIRD PATTERNS APPLIQUÉD BORDER UNIT A AND CENTER UNIT

Margaret Docherty

pink rose

LITTLE BROWN BIRD PATTERNS APPLIQUÉD BORDER UNIT B

Margaret Docherty

Alternate Bow

If you have, as I did, to extend the length of the appliqué borders because of "shrinkage," the corner ivy wreath will appear too open. To fill it in, use the alternate bow and appliqué a small green and brown bird (pages 65) at the open top edge of the wreath. Brown stems below the blue bow can be adjusted as necessary.

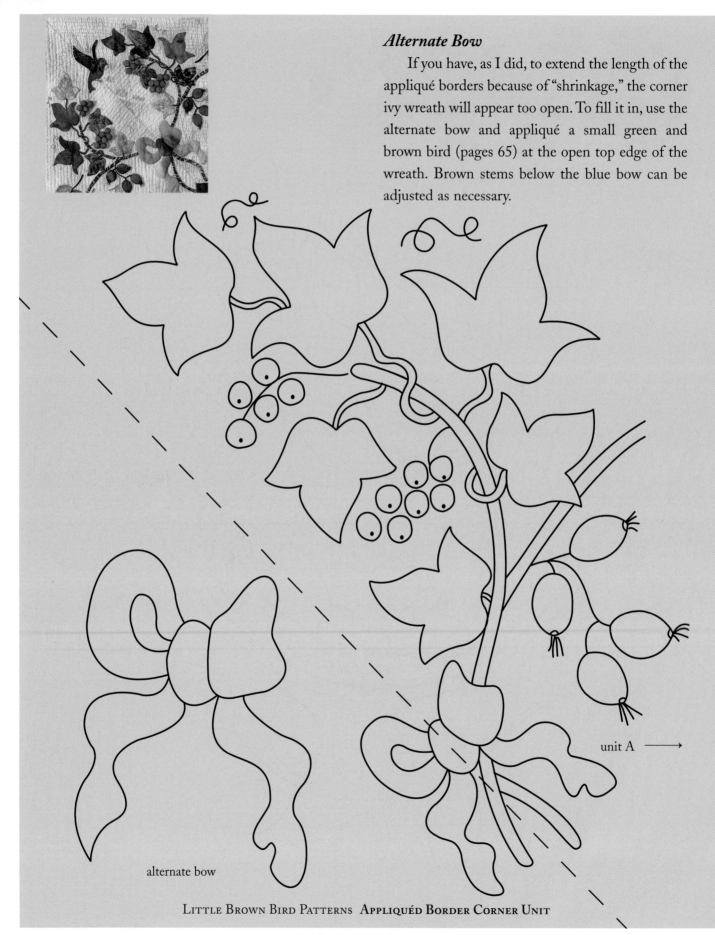

alternate bow

unit A ⟶

LITTLE BROWN BIRD PATTERNS APPLIQUÉD BORDER CORNER UNIT

Margaret Docherty

CHAPTER 6

Quilt Assembly

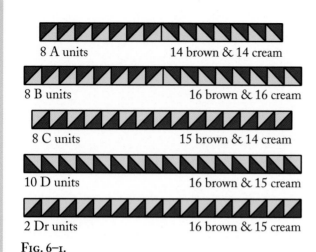

8 A units   14 brown & 14 cream

8 B units   16 brown & 16 cream

8 C units   15 brown & 14 cream

10 D units   16 brown & 15 cream

2 Dr units   16 brown & 15 cream

Fig. 6–1.

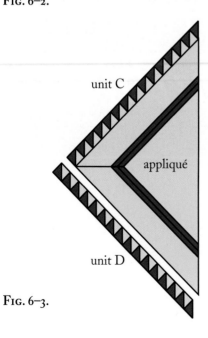

unit A

unit B   unit B

appliqué

unit A

Fig. 6–2.

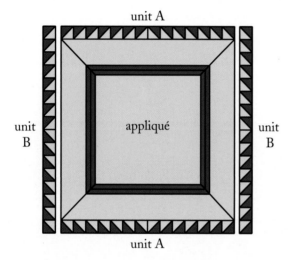

unit C

appliqué

unit D

Fig. 6–3.

Sawtooth Sashings

Join the half-square triangles to make the following units (Fig. 6–1):

❖ 8 Unit A

❖ 8 Unit B

❖ 8 Unit C

❖ 10 Unit D

❖ 2 Unit Dr

If you are familiar with foundation piecing, this is the most accurate way to assemble the sawtooth sashings.

Block Assembly

1. Make 40 8½" appliqué blocks.

2. Join 36 blocks in groups of four to form nine 16½" square units.

3. To the remaining four blocks (13, 14, 27, and 28), add sashings in the following order: blue, brown, and cream. Miter the corners.

4. To opposite sides of each block, attach two Unit A sawtooth borders with the points of the brown triangles facing inward (Fig. 6–2).

5. To remaining two sides, attach Unit B sawtooth borders, again with points of brown triangles facing inward (Fig. 6–2).

6. Add the blue, brown, and cream sashing to the eight half blocks and four quarter blocks as previously described.

7. Attach a sawtooth Unit C as shown in Fig. 6–3, with the points of the brown triangles facing inward.

8. Complete the side triangles by stitching a Unit D as shown. To complete the corner triangles, add a D or Dr unit as shown in Fig. 6–4.

Quilt Assembly

Assemble the quilt as follows:

1. Sew units together to form diagonal rows as shown in Fig. 6–5.

2. Sew the diagonal rows together.

3. Attach narrow brown and blue borders and miter the corners.

4. Attach the appliquéd border and miter the corners. (Refer to instructions for the border appliqué, pages 130–131, for accurate sizing of this border.)

5. Attach the outer blue and brown borders and miter the corners.

If you prefer, each border can have its five strips sewn together and added to the quilt as one single unit.

6. When all borders are sewn in place and the corners are mitered, complete the corner appliqué (see pattern and instructions for border appliqué, pages 130–134).

7. Ensure that all water-erasable markings are removed from the completed quilt top and press carefully.

The Quilting Pattern

You are now ready to mark your quilting pattern. Mark the quilt top before you sandwich the three quilt layers together. Handle the quilt top with care to avoid creasing.

I used a feathered design for the 2" cream sashings and stuffed this quilting by using the trapunto technique with a long needle and quilting wool.

FEATHER PATTERN

This was the only quilting marked. The blocks and borders were outline quilted around the appliqué, and the background was filled in with "off straight" lines between ⅛" and ¼"

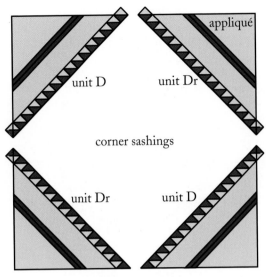

cut off small triangles that extend past the edges

FIG. 6–4.

FIG. 6–5.

FIG. 6–6. Appliqué Feather Block

FIG. 6–7. Scherenschnitte 2 Block

apart to give a rustic effect. For blocks 13, 14, 27, and 28, a different technique was used to produce a stipple effect. The blocks were echo quilted ¼" between the lines of quilting. The same line was then followed between the rows of quilting. Once the echo quilting lines are less than ¼" apart, the echo effect is lost and a stipple effect obtained. In this case, the rows are ⅛" apart (Figs. 6–6 and 6–7).

You may prefer to use a cross-hatch or other pattern for the background. Mark it along with the feathers.

Quilt Sandwich

A 100% cotton batting was used for LITTLE BROWN BIRD, and 3 yds. (2.5 m) of a 108" wide unbleached calico was used for the lining. If you use a 44" wide lining, you will need 8¼" yds. (7.5 m). Join the lining in three vertical panels with ¼" seams pressed to one side (Fig. 6–8).

Assemble the three layers of the quilt on a large flat surface. Start with the lining wrong side up. Smooth out wrinkles and hold down with tape (or pins if you are using a floor with carpet) at the edges. Next add the batting. Again, lay it flat, and smooth out all wrinkles. Finally, lay out the quilt top right side up, and smooth it out evenly.

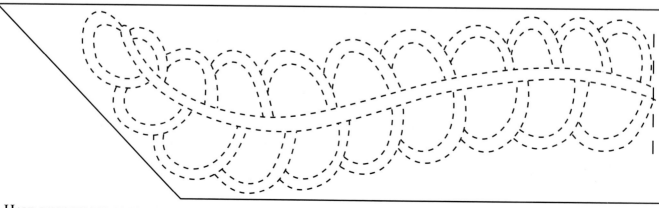

HALF-PATTERN FOR FEATHER QUILTING ON SASHING

Margaret Docherty

Use quilting pins to hold the quilt layers together and baste the layers in a grid fashion, using a strong thread such as quilting cotton (Fig. 6–9). Hand quilting may take several months to complete and fine threads may snap. to baste the layers, try to use a thread that matches your background. Dark threads may rub and leave dye marks on a light surface.

When the quilt sandwich has been basted, the batting and lining can be tidied up at the edges. Trim the batting so it projects beyond the quilt top by about ½" to ¾". Don't trim the quilt to its final size just yet. Several months of handling the quilt during quilting may cause some wear and tear to the edges. Trim the lining about 1½" beyond the edge of the quilt top, turn in the raw edges and fold the extra fabric over to the right side of the quilt. Baste firmly in place along all four edges to protect all raw seam edges during the quilting process.

The Binding

When quilting is complete, remove all basting threads carefully. With dense quilting, many quilting stitches may be caught in the basting, and a careless approach to pulling out the basting might pucker or even tear your quilting. Trim your quilt edges neatly.

I leave ¼" on the quilt top, which is pre-planned during the construction of the top, but I leave slightly more than this on the seam allowance of the lining and on the batting. This excess seam allowance is used as a stuffing to give the binding a well-filled appearance, almost as if it were piped.

Lay the quilt out on a flat surface, such as a floor, and measure it. Measure all four edges as well as four horizontal and four vertical lines through the body of the quilt.

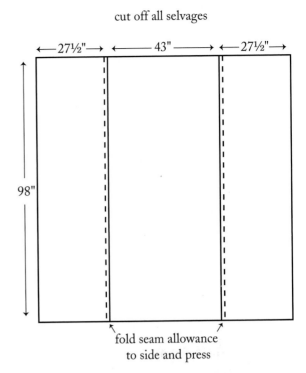

cut off all selvages

←—— 27½" ——→ ←——— 43" ———→ ←—— 27½" ——→

98"

fold seam allowance
to side and press

FIG. 6–8.

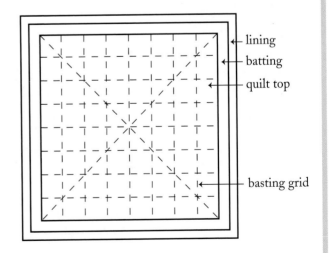

lining
batting
quilt top

basting grid

FIG. 6–9.

My version of LITTLE BROWN BIRD measured 90" x 90" before quilting, but after quilting, it had shrunk to 84¼" long and 84" wide.

Find the average measurements for the length and width and cut bindings these lengths. For a double bias binding, you will need twice the length, plus twice the width, plus ½" for start and finish turnings, plus 4" for the corner miters. Be generous – cut a little extra just in case. A very narrow double bias is difficult to work with, so you may want to cut yours 1⅞".

Fold the binding in two, wrong sides together and press. Stitch the raw edges to the right side of the quilt with a ¼" seam. Remember, at the corners, a miter is needed for both the front and back of the quilt. Fold the binding over and blind stitch the binding to the wrong side of the quilt just beyond the binding seam line.

Because my binding is well-stuffed, there is a degree of tension on my blind stitching. I tend to use a strong thread, such as quilting cotton, to blind stitch my binding in place.

Don't forget to add a label providing the name of the quilt, name of maker, address of maker, and completion date.

I added a logo to the label – the center motif from the border and the nursery days song that inspired the title.

If you plan to exhibit your quilt, remember to sew a 4" sleeve close to the top edge.

Mitering Borders

The inner edge of a border will have a finished length the same as that of the quilt body to which it is attached. The outer finished length will extend beyond this length by the width of the border *at each end*. Example: For a 70" wide quilt with an 8" border, the finished outer edge will be 86".

Mark the corner seams on each border as follows:

1. On the wrong side of the borders, measure in ¼" from the edges to mark the seam lines at both ends, as shown below. Mark off a square at each end. The square is equal to the width of the border, 8".

2. Check the distance between A-A and B-B on each border strip. A-A should be 70", and B-B should be 86".

3. Mark diagonal A-B lines as shown. These are the stitching lines.

4. Join all four borders to the quilt between points A-A.

5. To complete the border, joins seams A-B to A-B on adjacent borders.

6. Trim away excess fabric and press seam allowances to one side.

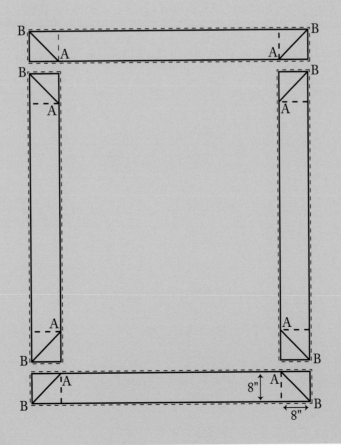

Bibliography

Sienkiewicz, Elly. *Dimensional Appliqué*, C&T Publishing, 1993.

Sienkiewicz, Elly. *Baltimore Album Quilts*, C&T Publishing, 1990.

Sienkiewicz, Elly. *Baltimore Beauties and Beyond*, C&T Publishing, 1991.

Hatcher, Irma-Gail. *Conway Album Quilt*, American School of Needlework, Inc., 1992.

Shackelford, Anita. *Three Dimensional Appliqué and Embroidery Embellishment*, American Quilter's Society, 1994.

Johnston, Ann. *Dye Painting!*, American Quilter's Society, 1992.

Rodgers, Sue H. *Trapunto*, Moon over the Mountain Publishing Co., 1990.

About the Author

Margaret Docherty, who was born in Hartlepool, England, learned to sew as a child. She became interested in quilting in the late 1980s and was greatly influenced by the work and writing of American quilters. Her main interest is in traditional hand appliqué, but she has experimented with most techniques and styles.

She makes time to quilt from her busy schedule as a pediatrician by sewing mostly at night – a legacy from her days as a junior hospital doctor. She enjoys teaching quilting as a change from teaching young doctors and medical students.

Margaret has won many awards at major shows both in England and the United States. She is particularly proud of the ribbons that LITTLE BROWN BIRD has collected, including the Gingher Award at the American Quilter's Society Show in Paducah, Kentucky, and Best of Show at the International Quilt Festival in Houston, Texas.

Other AQS Books

This is only a small selection of the books available from the American Quilter's Society. AQS books are known worldwide for timely topics, clear writing, beautiful color photos, and accurate illustrations and patterns. The following books are available from your local bookseller, quilt shop, or public library.

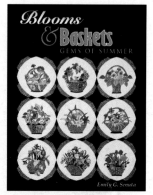

#5175 $24.95

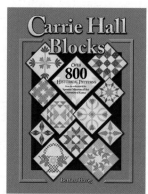

#4957 (HB) $34.95

#4833 $14.95

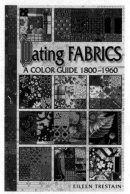

#4827 (6" x 9") $24.95

#4898 $16.95

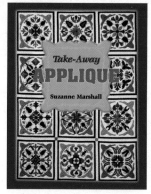

#5012 $22.95

#4830 $19.95

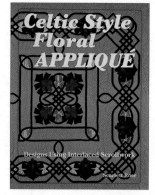

#3926 $14.95

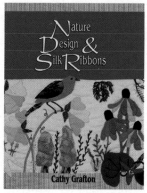

#4828 $18.95